RIVERWISE

Jack Smylie Wild is a poet, nature writer and award-winning baker. Born in Aberystwyth in 1989, but mostly raised on the edge of Dartmoor, he has been moving between Wales and England for thirty years. It was from his home in Buckfastleigh that as a teenager Jack began wandering, and writing about, the moors and its rivers. He has been captivated by wild spaces ever since, and in 2011 won the Write It, Make It Happen award, which financed an expedition to Central America to write a collection of poetry about the remote cloud forests of Nicaragua. After studying philosophy at Cardiff University, he made a permanent return to his country, and county, of birth, settling in Llandysul with his partner Seren. It was here, jobless and with time on his hands, that he began to heed the calls of Afon Teifi – to explore her length and breadth; her creatures and her catchment. Jack now resides in Cardigan, with his wife and two boys, a stone's throw from the river he loves.

RIVERWISE

Meditations on Afon Teifi

JACK SMYLIE WILD

ILLUSTRATIONS BY IAN PHILLIPS

Parthian, Cardigan SA43 1ED
www.parthianbooks.com
First published in 2020
This edition 2021
© Jack Smylie Wild 2020
ISBN 978-1-913640-39-2 print
ISBN 978-1-912681-90-7 ebook
Editor Carly Holmes
Cover art and internal illustrations by Ian Phillips
Cover design by Syncopated Pandemonium
Map by Lisa Hellier
Typeset by Elaine Sharples
Printed by 4Edge Limited in the UK
Published with the financial support of the Books Council of Wales
British Library Cataloguing in Publication Data
A cataloguing record for this book is available from the British Library.

for my parents
who showed me the way;
for those teachers
who believed in my words;
and for Jolyon Parish, also,
who wanders the wild lanes

*...Remember the small
secret creases of the earth – the grassy,
the wooded, the rocky – that the water
has made, finding its way...*[1]

WENDELL BERRY

[1] Wendell Berry, *This Day: Collected and New Sabbath Poems, 1979-2013* (Berkeley: Counterpoint, 2014), p.100.

CONTENTS

....

INTRODUCTION

....

This isn't a traditional river book: it doesn't tie history and scholarship into an ordered, geographically straightforward account of the Teifi's course. I tried, once, to write such a book – but the voice that came through wasn't my own. So I wrote this – a description of how my life is bound to, and entangled within, the currents of a river I love.

In 2012 I moved west to settle in Llandysul, where my partner lived. I was lost, jobless; I had no car, no knowledge of where I had landed; I was yet to make friends; I lacked purpose and motivation. Then, one day, the river called me. It asked me to find out where it came from, where it was headed. (Years later the river would encourage me to ask the very same questions of myself.) I searched for sources and endings to see what they could tell me. I stared at water and wondered what it was. And then I heard the river speak again. Look beyond the water, beyond the banks – look at the life, and the lives, that arise here.

If this book, then, grew out of a yearning for topographical and spiritual connection, in the end its words arose as a hymn to those liminal, fluvial places where one glimpses with astonishment the secret, unfolding moments of an enchanted universe. And if I began this exploration with a heavy leaning toward the ontological mysteries of water itself, eventually my obsession centred around the context of water – that is to say, the landscapes through which it winds its way, the lives it passes by, the moments idled away in its presence. In this way, after years of Teifi-focussed wanderings, I began to turn more and more toward those tributaries and their valleys which fuel the Teifi – those secret springs and rivulets and streams which are, literally, its lifeblood. Three such streams, and their landscapes, emerged as places of deep importance to me – that is, as friends, as sanctuaries.

As with most relationships, the process of befriending the Teifi wasn't a linear affair – instead, it took place across disparate times and places. I came to know her over many years, by exploring her context, contours and catchment in a somewhat erratic manner. The side effect of this is that the seasons, and sometimes years taken as wholes, are jumbled up into a mishmash of "Teifi time", jerking, sometimes obviously and at others more subtly, hither and thither against a backdrop of more ordered geographical progression. This is, after all, how we ourselves play out our lives – moving forward, yes, but also skipping ahead, retreating back, mixing time and place in currents of re-membering and dreaming.

And it happens that I began life by the Teifi, in her sur-rounding valleys and hills. I never set out to incorporate memoir into this account, but as the years went by – and I realised more and more that this book was to be a tale of friendship, as much about myself as it is about Teifi – it came to seem important to relate certain aspects of my own life which are intertwined with her currents and her country. Acquainting myself with Teifi's landscape, it turned out, was to inadvertently begin a process of refam-iliarisation with my own past. Four years in, it occurred to me that one tributary in particular, high in the hills, needed to be revisited, and had hitherto remained mysteriously absent from my writing and radar. Old questions and some new answers, neglected throughout the entire course of this journey, were waiting for me there.

The book also represents a searching for some kind of answer to a question Seamus Heaney poses at the end of his poem, 'A Herbal':

Where can it be found again,
An elsewhere world, beyond

Maps and atlases,
Where all is woven into

And of itself, like a nest
Of crosshatched grass blades? [2]

---

[2] Seamus Heaney, *Human Chain* (London: Faber & Faber, 2010), p.43.

A WARNING

No one will teach you your land – not in its full, hidden charm; not in the secret ways it can become your own: you must journey out, alone, seeking those forgotten places where pieces of your total self dwell, lying in wait, residing in the form of a gorse-covered slope, in the bend of a lonely brook, in the view of the high moor curving into the sky. At first you might not realise that you are seeking and finding pieces of the puzzle of the self; after all, you are discovering the intricacies and intimacies of an outer realm too. But upon returning home, you feel how knowing the land is also to acquaint yourself with that vaster body, or being, which you, in small but glorious part, form.

CATCHMENT, CENTRE, SOURCE

"Of al the pooles, none stondith in so rokky and stony soile as the Tyve doth, that hath withyn hym many stonis. The ground al about Tyve, and a great mile toward Stratfler*, is horrible with the sight of bare stones, as Cregeryri Mountains be. Llin Tyve is in cumpase a iii quarters of a mile, being ii miles est from Strateflere. It is fedde fro hyer places, with a little broklet, and issueth out again by a small gut. There is in it very good trouttes and elys, and noe other fisch..." [3]
*Strata Florida Abbey

Sometimes the source beckons, and suddenly I am driving the fifty winding miles from the mouth of the river to the place, high in Elenydd, where the Cambrian hills give birth to many springs. I travel up the coast road, and then pass inland, over Mynydd Bach – the bleak moorland where I spent the first few years of my life.

[3] John Leland, *The Itinerary in Wales of John Leland* (1536-1539), quoted by J G Wood in *The Principal Rivers of Wales* (London, 1813), p.139.

As I drive along the twisting, familiar lanes of this small wilderness – where the weather rules supreme – I move backwards in time as I pass the landscape of my childhood: feral sheep; lichen-flecked walls; lakes – or *llyns* – like the crystal eyes of the hillsides; abandoned, graffitied bus stops; petrol stations fit only to refuel rusty Morris Minors and antique tractors; lonely shacks sheltered by a single tree, surrounded by decaying vehicles, their yellow paint flaking to reveal the rust that will return them to the ground; tussocks of grasses, rushes and sphagnum mosses that ooze an earthy, damp perfume.

It seems to me that anyone who spends time getting to know this range of hills between the Cambrians and the coast will fall for it in a profound way. Gwyn Williams, writer and translator of Welsh poetry, was one such inhabitant of Mynydd Bach. He lived for many years near its centre, and his deep bond to the area is recorded in his *Summer Journal 1951*.

Before settling on the moorland permanently, he would spend his summers in the isolated cottage of Blaenbeidog, near Trefenter, with his wife Daisy, a textile artist and painter. Between his translation work and visiting Aberystwyth to socialise and go to the National Library, he spent his days hunting wildfowl, fishing and birdwatching, as well as partaking in the more pragmatic affairs of cutting peat, harvesting oats and making hay with his old friend, and second cousin, Dai Morus.

His diary entry for Saturday the 4th of August describes a typical summer day for Gwyn, although his sighting in the evening sky was presumably a less ordinary occurrence:

"Helped Dai Morus with some rough hay and went shooting with him after supper. We did the usual pools and bits of bog and put nothing up. Dai got a teal at a pool beyond Garn Wen but the mountain was very quiet. The curlew seem to have gone. A lovely evening with a wild sky... on the way home we saw a flying saucer, or what has come to be called so. It was fairly high in a clear patch of sky to the north-west... it shone like polished silver, was very slim and slightly curved on the top side... It gave me the impression of being extremely far away, but it was quite distinct in the sky." [4]

These days the hills here harbour a new cast of characters. Tucked away on a lonely hillside, in an ancient, rusting school bus, lives our old friend Greg. Biker, hippy, wild man, bearded recluse – none of these epithets do justice to the individual who has made this place his home, by dwelling here quietly, under the radar, for thirty or so years in order to lay claim to this small patch of Mynydd Bach. On the face of it, he probably epitomises the kind of person more traditional folk such as Gwyn would have frowned upon; would have even feared perhaps. But Greg has become as much a part of this wild land as Gwyn or any of his forebears; has come to understand and love it in his own way just as deeply.

....

[4] Gwyn Williams, *Summer Journal, 1951* (Aberystwyth: Planet Books, 2004), p.24.

And while Gwyn and Dai took pleasure in hunting the wild creatures that abounded in the forests, bogs and fields here – thus cutting their lives short – Greg has set up a makeshift sanctuary for the wounded animals he sometimes chances upon on the moor or in the lanes that meander about these quiet hills. When I stop by, he is caring for a buzzard and a fox, which otherwise would have perished from their human-inflicted injuries.

We sit out in the hot sun in front of his antique bus and stare at the distant glistening of Cardigan Bay. 'This is what it's all about,' he muses. 'People are welcome to come here and enjoy it, but if they're arseholes, they can piss off.' Driving on to my destination, these words echo round my head. I found out two years later that he'd been diagnosed with a ferocious form of lung cancer just before I visited him; he literally didn't have time for people – who lacked respect for this land – to get in the way of his connection to it. When death is on your doorstep, anything that threatens to get in the way of raw life is unwelcome. Greg and Gwyn aren't so different after all, I think: both want visitors to respect their home and their way of life.

Two years before this particular trip to Greg, I happened to consider my own (inevitable) death in relation to this elemental landscape of stone, water, wind and light:

I will die,
Fulfilled or not so much –
Or somewhere in between.
But the smells of Mynydd Bach will endure –
Those damp perfumes of rain-hammered moor
And water-logged moss
And the base note which strikes a deep chord
And cannot be named –
Cannot be found elsewhere.

The scent of dark pine plantations,
Of nibbled grass and sheep shit –
These come and go;
But always the odour of earth,
Of its peat and its plants,
Of the life and the light
That grow from the dirt and the dead.

When I die this smell will be the last thread
Of my spirit to linger here,
Before dispersing into unknown ethers.
It will depart after my other senses
Have thrown up the place,
Conjured Mynydd Bach in the mind of a man dying:

A row of gnarled beeches,
Like a many-legged beast,
Arching down the hillside
To sip from a llyn –
Eiddwen or Fanod,
Whose waters lap the shore,
Ruffled into waves
By the wild west wind.
The birds here
Suddenly ascend –
The grey gulls,
The heron, the nervous flock of lapwings;
The swallows above the glistening water
Rising higher,
And way up, in the cloud almost,
A red kite spiralling.

I will glimpse the things men made –
Tools to tame a wasteland,
Walls to hold a home,
Ravaged by the elements.
The ruined shacks and crumbling stone of cottages,
Where a holly grows through a chimney
And an ash climbs through a window;
The rusting gates, the rotting stiles,
The fences succumbing to the ground
And the grind of the long winters.

And then the view from Hafod Ithel,
Shared one hazy evening with my father,
Of all Ceredigion.

And then the smell of death and life,
That damp perfume of Mynydd Bach.

I was two years old when we moved to the parcel of land below Llyn Eiddwen, where Greg now lives. My father was twenty-six and my mother twenty-five. Who were we then, that young family, living in an old brown and cream Bedford ambulance halfway up the hillside? Only three short decades have passed since we called that place our home, and that humble manner of subsistence our way of life, and yet it seems another world, another age. My own boys are growing fast and so I inevitably compare and contrast the first few years of their lives with my own: they have begun life within the four walls of our own house; I started out in caravans and trucks and makeshift benders of hazel and tarpaulin; whilst we have steady jobs, my parents were skint, on the dole, doing odd-jobs. And if there's any hint of implicit hierarchy or judgment in these comparisons, then this is not my intention. I emerged into a different world and would have it no other way. They have started here, with us, and so it is meant to be.

I thank my parents for the unwavering philosophy of freedom they lived by in those uncertain years. I thank them too for the courage of their convictions, and for giving their child everything he needed when, in a material sense, they owned basically nothing at all. They learnt, and so taught me, that there isn't much we truly need if love moves unencumbered, and unhurried, between us; if our spirits remain vital.

How did they come to Mynydd Bach, to a hill near Trefenter, those lost, beautiful young hippies? They have their stories – both followed friends who had moved to Aberystwyth to attend university. Yet there is also the story of the times – that landscape of culture and politics and generational friction – which can be seen as a backdrop to their westerly migration. Both were running from urban life in Thatcher's Britain; running too from the expectations of their middle-class families (who themselves had succeeded in climbing up and out of working-class toil and thus harboured certain assumptions that their children would aspire to maintain and build upon their own hard-won achievements – pursuing careers, working hard: being like them).

It was not meant to be. My mother travelled south-west from suburban Manchester, whilst my father journeyed north-west from Southampton. West Wales exerted its mysterious pull on those who were seeking to "turn on, tune in and drop out". "The System", so stifling in the cities, struggled to gain a foothold here and conquer the Welsh hills.

A decade or so earlier a slightly different crowd had been drawn out west, looking for a new way of life. Whereas my parents' generation came running, disillusioned –

pushed in a sense to the margins of the mainland – these older pioneers had set out with an arguably more positive impetus. John Seymour had published his array of "back to the land" literature, and so in the 60s and 70s the first hippies, inspired by his example, sought solitude and cheap, verdant land on which to fulfil their dreams of a self-sufficient "good life".

If Wales in general met a lot of their criteria for a certain kind of arcadia, it seems that the hills inland of Aberystwyth, and in particular the area of Mynydd Bach, became a stronghold for those misfits and unorthodox individuals – often artistic, eccentric – who together comprised a motley crew that sought a different kind of life.

Such was the west-Walian scene then – a hybrid and intermingling of earthy, settled older hippies on one hand and lost, itinerant young people on the other – often sharing similar ideals and philosophies, as well as a powerful propensity to party.

It's hard to imagine now in these quiet hills, here in Ceredigion's rural heartland. Beats blasting out of re-purposed small-holdings and lonely houses miles from anywhere, down bumpy tracks. Ounces of hash and copious quantities of tea shared around tables littered with rizlas and piles of esoteric tomes; outside, the wind howling and the rain driving across damp paddocks and dark clumps of conifer.

At Ffair-Rhos I turn off the main road and head along the snaking, single-track lane that will lead me into the heart of Elenydd. This bare, bulging moonscape of upland hills, which is generally taken to refer to the area lying between Pumlumon in the north and Mynydd Epynt in the south, is also known as the Desert of Wales. It's not a lack of rain, nor green, that gives it this name, far from it; rather, it's the fact of its desertion – its barrenness and remoteness; its unrelenting harshness.

I begin my climb, wondering what I might uncover about sources and their enigmatic beginnings. From a series of waterlogged plateaus above Llyn Teifi, the stream that feeds the lake at its northern-most point – Nant Rhydgaled – begins as barely more than a mineral-rich trickle in a peaty ditch, gurgling and pooling, hidden by grass.

Only metres away, a similar ditch grooves its way eastward to add its incremental flow to the waters of the young Afon Claerddu, which itself feeds the Claerwen Reservoir, a couple of miles to the south-east. Where the reservoir begins, Ceredigion ends, and gives way to the historic counties of Radnorshire on the northern bank and Brecknockshire on the southern bank, which together with Montgomeryshire comprise modern-day Powys. Water from here journeys two ways: some heads northward to Birmingham where it will quench the thirst of the city's millions; some flows on to join Afon Elan, which in turn will confluence with the Wye just south of Rhayader. Such similar beginnings – these two rivulets – such different journeys.

I place a small piece of quartz from the mouth of the Teifi on a ledge by a tiny waterfall at this source – a linking of its seventy-three, dreamy miles with an offering of stone, that overlooked element of rivers, as much a part of them as water.

Onwards over bog and hill, through wind and light; northwards, seeking a fictional location – a figment of the measuring mind: the very centre of Wales. I pass the waterfalls at Claerddu, which carve their way through ridges that contour the hill. Below me the stream will soon pass the isolated, eponymous farmstead, which is now a bothy. The year 1852 is carved into one of its cornerstones. The last time I stopped by, the bedroom floor was covered with torn-up playing cards and spliff butts.

I follow the rust-red bed of the Claerddu higher into the hills, grateful for its company and use as a guide. The space and emptiness here are sublime in the true sense of the word – terrifying, awe-inspiring. Even the Teifi Pools far below seem like safe, sheltered places compared to the vast plateau of Waun Claerddu, an ocean of infinite pale manes of long-dead sedges and cotton grasses.

It's early May. The skylarks are breeding and nesting, and the soft lambs are suckling their hardy mothers, the queens of these harsh hills. I reach the shores of Llyn Fyrddon Fach – the wind and sun painting its surface into an aurora borealis of racing ripple and shade-shifting blue. On a beach of silt and shingle at the northern end of the lake I find a petrified tree stump – god knows how old; there haven't been trees of this girth up here for hundreds, if not thousands, of years. I find another submerged branch. It looks solid and bronze-like, but is soft to the touch. Judging by the horizontal banding it's an ancient wild cherry. Remains of five-thousand-year-old pine trees were found in the peat on the shores of Llyn Teifi in 1951 – could this stump too be a remnant of the old wild-wood which once thrived up here before the hungry axe-heads of our forebears, and the sheep of countless generations, shaved this upland bare?

I think of Elzéard Bouffier, the shepherd in Jean Giono's short story *The Man Who Planted Trees*, who planted the greatest forest that never was – his precious oaks spreading from the pages to inspire countless rewilding projects across the globe. Could the barren plains of the lower Alps, where he carried out his boreal gift to the world, have once been more devoid of trees than the uplands here? It's hard to imagine.

I walk down to Llyn Fyrddon Fawr, a stone's throw away. On its bare, bilberry bush shores, when the wind eases, the frenzied yet tuneful internet-dial-tone-song of the skylarks electrifies the airwaves. At the base of the steep, heather-clad western shore I find a stunted, lone rowan, housing a large, abandoned nest in its small boughs. Inaccessible to sheep (a very rare bit of luck indeed up here), it's managed to avoid grazing, and has clung on with all its might to the peaty soil despite the ceaseless lapping of the ruffled lake's waves.

At the northern end of the lake, I reach a small, ditchy stream – Nant y Fagwyr. I follow this to its saturated source in a blanket of bog which forms a wide pass between slopes to either side. The earth is pockmarked with great potholes, where the fibrous, peat-rich soil seems to have simply subsided and sunken away. I walk on, navigating these giant craters and their high banks. The pass flattens out and the sky grows wide. I descend a little.

So this is it. On the windswept slopes of Banc Mawr – the very centre of Wales. This is my "figment of the measuring mind" – the corresponding point at which, were you to cut a two-dimensional shape of Wales from a piece of cardboard, the country would balance on the pin-prick tip of a pencil. A mathematical imagining, then; an exercise in mapping the mind on to the moor.

And what a moor it is. In the valley far below, a freckling of buildings: Cwmystwyth – once a hideout for those pushed to the margins of the "civilised" world. Off in the distance, over bulging hills and the great forests surrounding Pontarfynach – or "Devil's Bridge" – lie the brooding slopes of Pumlumon, where a giant is said to slumber.

It could have been anywhere, theoretically speaking, the centre of Wales; but really it had to be here, in these lonely bare hills – the home of sheep, kites, ravens and skylarks; by these lonely lakes and the old stones – Carreg Corneldrawallt, Carreg Bwlchllynfyrddon, Carreg Ddiddos (the latter of which means "Weatherproof Rock" – anything that might provide shelter up here is deserving of a name).

This centre is close, as well, to the sources of many Welsh rivers: less than four kilometres from the Teifi's source, and ten kilometres from the Tywi's; over on the slopes of the Pumlumon massif, the Severn (354km) and the Wye (216km) have their humble, hidden beginnings, as do the Rheidol (30.5km) and the Ystwyth (33km) – the latter two burning their candles at both ends in search of the sea; tumbling in crystal torrents down toward Cardigan Bay.

On a large, lichen-encrusted boulder which squats low in the nibbled grass, I place another stone from the Teifi's mouth – a small maroon pebble in the centre of a rock which lies at the centre of Wales.

A short distance away, I find a huge lump of quartz lodged in some collapsed peat and carry it to the cairn atop Bryn Dafydd. The wind is shrieking with such ferocity as I place it on the summit of the enormous rock-pile that for a moment a fear creeps inside me. My hands are stinging. I look down and realise that I've sliced the tips of my fingers open on the jagged crystal blades of the quartz. With blood on my hands and the wind like a daemon in my head on the wild summit, there is something almost sacrificial – or at least terrifying – about being up here.

If the mouth of the Teifi, where I live and work, stands for civilisation – for business and busyness and human con-structs – then these hills around the source of the Teifi have come to represent for me those things that lie at the other end of the spectrum: freedom from thought, a redis-covery of enchantment, a wilderness of mind born of a wildness of place; my animal self, unencumbered by obligation, organisation, authority; inhabiting for a brief time 'an elsewhere world, beyond maps and atlases...'; existing for the sheer joy of being here, at the source.

Far down below me now I can see the woods of the Hafod estate. In the late eighteenth century, Hafod became one of the most celebrated "picturesque" landscapes in Europe, and was also one of Wales's first major tourist attractions. Thomas Jones, a member of Parliament who inherited the estate from his father in 1780, set about moulding this wild upland area according to the latest aesthetic theories of landscape design. Between 1782 and 1813, he was responsible for the planting of over three million trees, as he sought to transpose and synthesise his ideals of "the beautiful" and "the sublime" upon the landscape. Hearing of this "arcardia", people flocked to Hafod to soak up its enchanting atmosphere. Even William Blake, the great luminary of the Romantic age, is said to have taken an interest in the place, possibly engraving the map in George Cumberland's 1796 book, *An Attempt to Describe Hafod*.

Down there, hidden in the dark, dripping trees, lies a special place for me: a jagged tunnel cut through rock deep into the wooded hillside leads to a waterfall inside the hill. Daylight, as well as water, pours down from the forest high above into the spray-filled, drumming hollow, from which the water urges forth through a narrow ravine, and out into the *cwm* beyond. When Seren and I visited recently during a particularly wet July, we were both dumbfounded by the thunderous force of the falls; as we moved slowly along the dripping tunnel toward the faint light beyond the bend, it was as if we were approaching a beast in its lair. The noise was deafening; the air so misty it seemed more liquid than gas. We talked about glimpsing something not meant to be seen; of viewing something from an impossible vantage point – of becoming like the stone itself, which had been cut away to create a window on to a secret world, on to the earth's deep secret; of an energy so wild and focussed it seemed sentient, divine – certainly sublime.

This is also a place of legend for me – the place where my dad dived into a seething torrent to rescue his dog Carlos, who had fallen from the slippery rim into the bubbling cauldron of frozen water below. As a child, I imagined them both being sucked down into dark tunnels, spinning and tumbling and drowning, descending into an abyss under the earth.

With mud and blood all over my hands, and no water left in my bottle, I descend south-west to a small mountain stream that will soon join Nant Gau. Here I strip off, wash and take my fill of the clear mineral waters. I climb up to Llan Ddu Fawr via the waterfalls of Nant Ffrwd-ddu. At 593 metres, it's the highest point for miles around – hence the Trig Point, which is enclosed by a cairn. The relentless wind invades my head yet again and blows away all thought.

Climbing back down to Claer-ddu, in the warm sun and the still ceaseless wind, a peace finds me; in the rhythm of walking, in the midst of these untamed elements, in the pure light and the pure air, in the simplicity of grazing ewes and lambs; in the wide vistas and the vast space; in the shivering of the soft-rush and the cotton-grass, a peace finds me, in these square kilometres, in this landscape, which is the centre, the very heart, of Wales.

As for the infant Teifi itself, which begins chartable life as a controlled trickle from the spillway of the Llyn Teifi dam, it's really just another mountain stream, descending rapidly down the "barren" moor of Cwm Teifi. After a couple of kilometres it merges with Afon Mwyro at Penddol Fawr before flowing past the ruins of Strata Florida Abbey. Atop the summit of a small hill near Troed-y-Rhiw, above this confluence, my dad – aged nineteen; stoned, tripping – spent weeks building a stone circle of river quartz. The grass and the years have reclaimed most of it now, but one giant crystal still sits at its centre.

In the intervening space between this confluence and the dam, the Teifi is joined by its first tributary after just a few hundred metres of life – a short-lived rivulet that originates from Llyn Pondygwaith and tumbles over a mossy ledge in a gully sheltered by a lone rowan, before it too gives up its waters to the young queen. In this mineral solution barely a foot wide, the first trout appear, the size of a child's finger, darting for cover.

Before long, the Teifi's first island has formed itself from boulders, upon which stubby bonsai heather hosts a wren, hopping into shadow. No animal wants to be seen up here, where everyone wants a free meal and no one wants to be one. Just a few hundred metres on, the trout have fattened in proportion to the rivulet, and now weigh about twenty-five grammes, reaching up to three inches in length. But don't let their meagre frame deceive you: they say these slippery black fish are as old the hills themselves – just like the Mabinogion's Salmon of Glynllifon: "I am as many years old as there are scales upon my skin, and particles of spawn within my belly."

Just beyond the island, protruding from a pile of stones on the bank, an ash has wound its way slowly up into the sky: the Teifi's first tree. The prolonged growth of any tree up here is an event of miraculous defiance in the face of the ubiquitous sheep. It is perhaps a hundred or even a hundred and fifty years old, and in its boughs are two nests: the lower and larger of the two, now a platform for moss and grass, has been crosshatched using fragments of barbed wire and nylon twine. The Teifi's first nest is a fortress; testament to the weather of Elenydd; symbol of the struggle to survive in these wild uplands.

Beyond the tree is a cairn – the first sign of human activity on the stream. Beside the glacial hunks of quartz and the lichened mudstones and siltstones, shards of asbestos piping – washed down from the dam – have been stacked. A fitting way to honour the land and our ancestors who dwelt in it, by making a mound from the things that pollute it; by removing poison from the water.

Half a kilometre on from the ash tree, the rivulet has grown in character. Its marginally faster, wider flow has oxygenated the water, allowing water-crowfoot and other aquatic plants to thrive; the first small gravel beds are also formed as a result of the torrent's newfound power.

Soon the swaying moorland grasses of Cwm Teifi will give way to the close-cropped green of civilisation's fringes. But before the young stream says farewell to the moor, it has at least one more surprise for those who come seeking topographical treasures: suddenly the tiny Teifi disappears silently over a ledge, an infinity pool that slides as a clear, thin film down steep, smooth bedrock.

STILL

....

Being still, in one spot, I witness the dance of the wind in the sycamore leaves which jostle in profusion; the coming and going and shifting of the light; the gentle glide of the clouds; the twig of ash which spins like the needle of a compass in a foam-filled eddy; the mysterious tangle and chaos of currents in a river which hardly seems to change.

I'm not the first to notice this paradox at the heart of the river's identity. Far from it. The philosopher Heraclitus, as far as we know, was the first to articulate the idea in writing around 500 BC: "Everything changes and nothing remains still... and... you cannot step twice into the same stream."

Poets and writers too have been moved by this peculiar quality – "the continual change of the Matter, the perpetual sameness of the Form", as Coleridge put it. Edward Thomas saw and expressed it thus in his poem 'The Brook':

> *"The waters running frizzled over gravel,*
> *That never vanish and for ever travel."* [5]

Byron, in his *Lara, A Tale*, finds a metaphor for the human condition in the movement of water:

> *"So calm, the waters scarcely seemed to stray,*
> *And yet they glide, like happiness, away."* [6]

And then there is Siddhartha, in Herman Hesse's eponymous novel, who recognised that water was always the same and yet continually renewed. Failing to resolve this dichotomy intellectually, the young man realises that this liquid paradox somehow points toward the divine.

Talking of which, it is the "divine voices" – the layered music – of the Teifi valley that I now become aware of: the drill of a distant woodpecker, the whisper of the wind in the reeds, the grind of an underwater boulder, the bleating of the fat lambs across the river.

Later in the day I come across a passage by N S Momaday, in a book Seren once gave me as a gift:

"Once in his life a man ought to concentrate his mind upon the remembered earth, I believe. He ought to give himself up to a particular landscape in his experience, to look it at it from as many angles as he can, to wonder about it, to dwell upon it. He ought to imagine that he

....
[5] Edward Thomas, *Edward Thomas: Everyman's Poetry* (London: Everyman Paperbacks, 1997), p.58.
[6] Lord Byron, *Lara, A Tale* (London: J Murray, 1814).

touches it with his hands at every season and listens to the sounds that are made upon it. He ought to imagine the creatures there and all the faintest motions of the wind. He ought to recollect the glare of noon and all the colours of the dawn and dusk." [7]

This, then, would be my mission – to touch the Teifi with my hands at every season, to listen to the sounds that are made upon her; to imagine her countless creatures, her infinite tremblings in the wind, her myriad appearances and apparitions.

[7] N Scott Momaday, *The Way to Rainy Mountain* (Albuquerque: University of New Mexico Press, 1969) p.83.

TRIBUTARY: NANT CLYWEDOG-ISAF

Following Nant Clywedog-isaf up the bed of the stream itself, high in forestry plantation, is novel at first: it winds through clearings no one, surely, has been to in a long time – not since these mossy, lichen-jewelled stumps were severed from the trees they anchored to the earth. The stream is small and clear, and apart from the occasional deep pool beneath a step in the bedrock, it is shallow enough to use as a pathway – indeed, it is the only clear route forward up these slopes into the high Cambrian moor. I find a few pieces of pottery – intriguing, seeing as there are no houses or old homesteads above me. The Romans who built Sarn Helen had a Practice Works up here, but my finds are far younger than that. They had their stories, once, these relics, but the Clywedog has long since scoured them off and carried them away.

The forestry opens out and allows the stream some breathing space. On either side it is now bordered by boggy, mossy heath with deer and fox tracks running through it, dotted with the odd bush of broom, stunted beech or deer-nibbled oak. The stream gurgles and slices through the sodden earth. Gradually it narrows, and becomes more of a ditch than a stream, so that the grasses on opposite banks sometimes entwine and crosshatch to conceal it, and the rivulet becomes nothing more than a watery sound, an underground song. The forestry narrows too, and soon it seems that the close-knitted pines on three sides of me will offer no exit – perhaps I will have to turn back. The going is tough now – brambles proliferate, the ground is pockmarked with bog and pools. My welly goes under. Decaying piles of discarded branches bar the way. This place does not afford human convenience – it is a place for plants, for streams; for deer, fox, woodcock and kestrel; for the lichen and moss, for the cold air and the wind; for the crumbling stone walls infringed upon by jostling pines.

As the cloud and mist draw in, I eventually find a track across the moor and cease to be lost. Trudging the puddled, stony way back to the lane my car is parked on, I reflect on these small journeys I make, and ask myself why I persist in exploring hidden landscapes. It's the promise of a find, I tell myself – of treasure, tangible or experiential – that keeps the walker, the writer, the seeker all moving forward, alert, like a hunter.

Such a search inevitably has plenty of room for frustration and disappointment. Later in the day, safely home, I find a sentence in my diary from another "tributary trip" which sums up the absurdity and sheer futility such outings can harbour: "I panned for gold in the Morgenau, and stood bewildered in the darkness which had crept up on me, wondering what it was I was searching for in this forgotten stream, far from home." Perhaps these journeys themselves are, in fact, a form of searching for "home"– inner or outer; inner *and* outer.

MUSE (OR, ADVICE TO A YOUNG POET)

On the last day of March, after a hard day's work, cycle out of town to a field overlooking your beloved river. Notice how spring stirs in the air, pulses in the bulging buds, soars in the flight of the first swallows that hunt in ecstasy above the pale reeds of the marsh. Notice all these things, breathe them in, feel the gorgeous air against your deprived face – but don't go too slowly; it is the last day of March, and the sun will soon slip behind that distant hill – in just over an hour, at 7:40pm.

I know – it's been a hard, long day. Work has tricks to make you stay too long. Cycle on, and find your spot – somewhere you feel safe, comfortable, at home; happy to be alone with your own strange thoughts; somewhere out of town, far from everything, but not too far.

Even as you crumple up newspaper for your fire, the world – the terrible world – will attempt in vain to entice you back into its web of information; ignore the headlines, the help columns, the eye-catching pictures: this is no place to pay attention to things distant from you. Pay attention, instead, to the wide sky, to the soft sound of the river, which is almost like a woman singing gently; pay attention to the song of the twilight birds and to the kindling you are selecting. Don't deceive yourself into thinking that any old piece will do; no, only the best should be selected for this fire – the first fire of spring.

Select well-seasoned ash, oak or beech, and pile the thin sticks thick about those balls of sorry news. One match should suffice, if placed at the heart of the matter. Don't pile the larger sticks and branches on too soon – develop the heart; then and only then will a sound blaze take told – a blaze worthy of tonight's guest.

Talking of which, when the embered heart is alive and well, and sending a steady stream of the lightest smoke up into the heavens, stoke the small fire with enough wood to a make a blaze large enough for two. Creating a friendly fire with generous flames is an invitation to your guest.

The other company you will enjoy tonight consists of the flames themselves and the blue of the sky, and both will fade and die away as all things do, but not before you have feasted on their light. Coax the fire into a veritable furnace with a soft but concentrated breath. Only the effects of your focussed exhalation should be heard – a gentle whooshing, an irresistible crackling – but not your breath itself.

Now that the fire is healthy and releasing a divine smell, you are permitted to relax. Remove the red wine from your bag and allow it to breathe and warm a little by the fire's edge. Feast again on the raw elements surrounding you. This is life. This turf beneath your feet, this clear air so sweet in your nostrils, this moment, at whose precious centre you, young poet, now dwell – already composing lines in your mind's mouth – testing the water, searching for a form, a context, an angle – searching for the Muse herself.

But search not. Merely sit, be still, and witness these first bubbles – these initial ideas – arising and popping across the membrane of the mind. The fire is cooking something, and it is not yet ready. These bubbles are the beginning of the boiling. Incubate all the raw inspirations, swelling in your young heart, in the heart of the roaring fire. Now is the time to take a sip of the wine. Taste it, truly taste it – just as you are tasting the essence of the evening itself through your heart.

I am so pleased, young poet, that you are sipping wine by a fire tonight, for so too am I. Let us raise a glass, then, to the Muse who is on her way; and a toast to us, as well, my friend – to those of us who step beyond the border of the town to these open fields where a sweet peace is found; to us who seek that sun-lit key in the hope of opening the sun; that river secret, in the hope of merging with the sea.

Now return to your fire, rekindle it, and be a proper host to Her, who right now is walking up from the river, through the darkening woods, to the light of this fireside. You have sought her for so long, along the entire length of this paradise river, and always she has slipped round the bend as a shadow on the silken surface, or as a shifting of the light on the water. Now she has sought you out. Take the notepad from your bag, listen well and be Her scribe.

Write into the dark; jot away until you are unsure what shapes your letters are taking – just as I do. I cannot see what I am dictating. I can only hear Her in my ears, smell Her in the smoke of this fire, feel Her all about me in this heavenly dusk, inside my young heart as I scribble the last lines of my – Her – song...

To end at the ending
Is merely to end where the river is bending
And the river is bending beyond us for now
Yonder, full of wonders, full of songs,
Waiting for a lung and a tongue
To sing them aloud.

SALMON & WHISKY

....

It's April 1st, the beginning of the fishing season, and I head to Maesycrugiau to talk to Lewi Thomas, a native of the Teifi valley and veteran of Llandysul Angling Association. 'The thing about the Teifi is,' Lewi tells me as we sit down for tea (pronouncing the name of the river to rhyme with "ivy", as opposed to the way I say it which rhymes with "wavy"), 'it's a meandering river. There's always something fresh around the next bend. Not like the Tywi, the second longest river in Wales, which to my mind is straighter and has less trees on its banks.

'It's a special river,' he goes on, 'but not what it used to be.' He takes an album down from his shelf and slides out a few photos. 'That's me in '65, when we first moved here. You don't get salmon like that these days.' Strung up on a beam of wood between two farm buildings are six huge fish. Crouching beside his catch, with cap on and rod in hand, is Lewi as a young man. 'We used to get up to fifty salmon in a season,' he says, 'but we're lucky to get one nowadays. And we've got the graphs to prove it.'

Lewi owns the fishing rights to about 900 yards of pristine Teifi riverbank, and rents out a cottage to anglers who come to Maesycrugiau from far and wide. 'Every season since 1970 we've recorded our catches, so there's no disputing the decline, even though some will try to tell you that the fishing's fine.'

We step outside and admire the view of the river, which splits in two around Lewi's two-acre river island – making it the largest on the Teifi. 'You've come two months too late,' he says. 'The island was snowy with snowdrops. We've got a few clusters of rare hybrids down there as well, but I won't give you the exact location. I can't do anything on that island thanks to those flowers – apart from grow a few Christmas trees, but I've let them get too big now. You're welcome to go and have a look down there. It's a peaceful spot.'

Before I leave to explore the island, Lewi and his wife Velma show me the old pillbox next to his cottage. 'Now, I don't know if it's true,' he says, 'but I've heard that if Hitler had invaded Britain, he'd have landed in south Wales. So, to prepare for this they built pillboxes by all the bridges.' He opens the door. 'We use ours as a washroom now. Apparently, the Irish labourers who were building it sold the pieces of metal meant to reinforce it to local farmers.'

We walk back outside into the sun. 'These cottages used to be a public house within the Waunifor estate, which owned all the farms around here – about a thousand acres in total. But the lord of the estate, Alistair Lloyd, closed it down because he didn't like drink. But remember, Jack, nowhere in the whole of Ceredigion has more salmon and whisky been consumed than in my kitchen!'

In one of Alistair Lloyd's letters, I discover later, an intriguing literary link is made to the estate: "Waunifor was an old house possibly mentioned by Wordsworth, which has been enlarged from time to time." The "mention" which Lloyd writes about seems to refer to Ivor-Hall in the poem 'Simon Lee', which describes the trials and tribulations of a peasant huntsman:

"In the sweet shire of Cardigan,
Not far from pleasant Ivor-Hall,
An old man dwells, a little man,
Tis said he once was tall.
Full five and thirty years he lived.
A running huntsman merry;
And still the centre of his cheek
Is red as a ripe cherry." [8]

Well, this could easily have been written about Lewi Thomas, I think. A slight man, with rosy cheeks, a hunter of sorts, full of life, and full of love for the Teifi.

....
[8] William Wordsworth, 'Simon Lee' from *Lyrical Ballads* (1798).

ISLAND – JUNE

....

Whilst the world stays at home to watch the World Cup, I pack my sleeping bag, hammock, half a baguette I baked at 5am, some water and a kettle, and slip away to the river. In the empty streets there's a smell of fish and chips. I see a local fisherman entering The Porth as I pass, shirt freshly ironed – as at home in that pub as he is on the banks of the Teifi. Not me. There's only one place where I can feel at home on this summer evening.

When I checked the forecast a couple of hours ago, it promised soft sun and a hazy sky, but now I see a few heavy drops of rain dapple the river's calm surface as I leave the last of the houses behind on Cambrian Terrace. The air is warm and muggy, and some dark clouds are swelling high above.

This is my fiftieth trip to the river – Friday the 13th, and a full moon. The lanes are full of cow parsley and bramble flower, the last of the campions and thick waves of cleavers rolling ever higher into the hedges. The Teifi is low, so reaching my river island today is easy. The ale-brown, ankle-deep water, riffling in the shadows of alder, ash and willow, is surprisingly cool. As I feel my way across the shallows with my toes, I spy an up-bubbling in a deeper stretch. As the tiny stream of rising air starts to meander, I realise its source: an otter. I strain my eyes until the bubbles disappear, and wade on.

The island is at the apex of its summer transfiguration: shoulder-high nettles and clusters of white umbels disguise the familiar ground and conceal my usual route across this sparsely wooded teardrop of land which is about half an acre in size.

I move slowly, stinging myself nonetheless, and find a spot for the hammock at the stern of the island, in a raised clearing about four feet above water level. The riverbanks here are lined with bushy trees, so in the clearing I am doubly camouflaged.

There are only a handful of farms in this wide valley, but if I spy anyone on the mainland tonight, it'll be a fisherman stalking past the shadowy groves on the Carmarthenshire bank.

Both sides of the river are bordered by pasture: flat, expansive meadows in Ceredigion, rising up to the domed, wooded hill of Coed Y Foel. Around its summit, at 254 metres, lies the great circular ditch and scarp of an Iron Age hillfort. A bronze collar, made some time around the birth of Christ, was found in a hillside quarry there in 1896. Lush green slopes pocketed with copse and gorsey scrub lie on the Carmarthenshire side of the island.

The golden sun illuminates a pool beside my bedroom, which is fed by a small channel of water flowing through a gateway of rushes, and is hidden from passers-by by a small reed-covered gravel bed. Looking up through the gateway from my tree-stump perch, I see a wide, idle stretch of river, framed by oak and willow on either side, and by a distant hill of conifers above a bend in the river.

Round the corner come a gang of Canada geese – three families raising their young together. The parents jerk their heads about, always on guard, as the month-old goslings peck away at willow buds dangling above the water.

Small brown trout jump and plop in the last of the sun. Landing beside me, a dipper frightens itself and darts off, chirping its warning and disgruntlement to the twilight. The sun sinks behind the great hill, and I leave my seat to explore the island's crepuscular scenes.

Through a digital recording device I amplify the evening's sounds. The clarity of the birdsong is superb; it's set against a backdrop of river-sound: the trickle, gurgle and gloop of water, and the grind of stone. I hear a plane over-head and imagine that I'm deserted on an isolated island out to sea, and that the plane is searching for me, but I don't want to be found.

Then I hear what sounds like faint human voices in con-versation. Or is it just the river – talking to me? I've been awake since 3am, so my mind might be playing tricks. I tell myself that rivers can sound like people, and go off in search of firewood.

I build a circle of river stones in the clearing and, kneeling beside it, I scrape a rod of steel with a shard of flint. The task is to aim the resulting sparks of molten metal on to a pile of tinder to create an ember which can be coaxed into flame. My tinder consists of a feather stick I have whittled down with my Opinel, leaving curls of fine shavings attached at one end like unfurling petals. The dusky clearing flickers and flashes as I scrape away, but the strips of wood won't catch.

I strike away madly in the growing dark, fumbling for kindling and blowing on tiny embers with a gentleness that belies my slightly crazed state. Imagining a riverside passer-by being bemused by the intermittent illuminations in the heart of the dark island, I picture myself as a druid, or wizard, performing a ritual, casting spells; summoning the spirits of the ancients, worshipping the elements.

After an hour I give up – defeated – and reach for the newspaper and matches. Instant fire seems like a cop-out, but it's 10:30pm now, and with the dark finally upon me and the temperature dropping, I'm grateful for the flames, whatever their origin.

I'm sweating from my fire-lighting workout, stinking of woodsmoke and covered in stings and bites, but it feels good to be amid the raw elements, to feel their effects on my skin, to sense their unadulterated being, to be in the midst of a "non-human" place, and as such to feel my own being drawn closer to the pure life of nature.

I put the kettle by the fire and wait for the moon to appear. Although it's only just got dark, once the moon is out the night will brighten again. Then at 3am the first faint smudges of sunlight will leak back into the sky, dying it pale, until the great star eventually rises at 5am and splashes the world with its honey-hued light.

As the round moon rises above a hill, shining its white light down on me like a torch to see who is out at this hour, I begin to drift off, cosy in the warmth of the radiating stones, lulled to sleep by the harmony of the river's many songs.

ISLAND – AUGUST

....

Back on my island, I leave the rest of the world and its worries – and my worries – behind. Here in the heart of the river I leave all paths and man-made things on the other shore. I have waded across the slowly rising waters of early autumn in the shadows of the trembling trees to a secret haven, to a small wilderness. I am an alien landing on an unknown planet, frozen by its quiet beauty, trying to read its cryptic language of leaf and stone and print and river song. The tightness in my chest eases and my lungs breathe deep in the cool air.

I have come back to explore, to experience the many changes of this microcosm, to hide amid the hogweed and the balsam, to merge into the green, to wait for the blue of the kingfisher to cast its spell on me and carry away any residue of disenchantment and dullness upstream and into the ether, like a small grey fish in its talons, as it darts into its hidden universe; to sit still and magnetise the sheen of an otter's curving back to the spot of dark and silver water which scurries beneath the leaf-laden alders, sycamores and willows. I have come here to forget myself; to become, for an hour, another natural aspect of the river's gestalt.

Across the river from me, on the mainland, the cobnuts on the hazels are plump, the sloes are ripening fast into orbs of dark purple, and the elderberries, a similar colour, aren't far behind. Blackberries are clustering in the lanes. The heavy tangles of vegetation on the island, nestled beneath the tall trees, are starting to thin out and collapse under their own turgid weight. Leaves are beginning to fall. On the log that hosted oyster mushrooms late last autumn, other fungi are emerging for their allotted period of spore dispersal. The temperature has dropped sharply in the last couple of weeks, especially at night, when two duvets are now required in our cold, old house. The light too is changing, becoming paler, somehow colder, eliminating distances and focussing the foreground in a bright sharpness. As light – the medium of vision – fades, we turn to things closer to hand, and hold our gaze upon ourselves perhaps.

Having explored the island, I sit down on a log beside an inland channel of water and watch the ripples caused by small trout as they rise. I think about my life; about where I'm going next, if I'm ready for it; if I want it. I eat some oatcakes and cheese and then get up to visit the island's stern. Under a huge nest of driftwood I find a dense cluster of spraint – one deposit still wet and shiny. An otter has been here very recently. A dark shadowy nook far back in the tangle of sticks looks like the opening to a holt.

On the island's portside I spy a tree leaning out over the river. It's an ash, torrent-toppled, now grown strong in its repose. I climb along its mossy trunk right out above the middle of this side of the river, and lie belly-down, gazing upstream to a wide, mirror-still stretch, bordered on all sides by trees. In a nearby oak a crowd of long-tailed tits flits from branch to branch like a gang of excitable children. I could lie here all day, some strange sloth-like creature stretched out along a leaning trunk, gazing at the water of the enigmatic river running ceaselessly seaward. 'What is a river?' I ponder, not for the first time. A word that crossed my mind earlier bubbles up into consciousness: gestalt – the river is other than the sum of its parts; a complex, multi-layered pattern of processes we perceive as a whole. And beyond language, it is this moment, beneath me, before and behind me, flowing on, sustaining life.

I say farewell to the island and wander home in the dusk, through the quiet meadows to the dark stream of tarmac which will carry me back to the human world.

MISFITS, MAGIC & TIME

....

"At some stage during this [late Tertiary/early Quaternary] period, both the Afon Rheidol and Afon Ystwyth, experiencing their own episodes of rapid downcutting, captured the northern headwaters of the proto-Teifi. The large river which had cut the broad lower reaches of the Teifi valley was thus much reduced in size and that which remains, sourced from Llyn Teifi, is a misfit river." [9]

I too am a misfit, and the sound of my own name has at times been a source of surprise. When I moved to Llandysul in 2012, I went to register with the local GP. 'We already have a Jack Smylie Wild on our system,' said the woman behind the desk in her lovely Ceredigion accent. 'He registered with us back in 1994.' For a moment I was baffled. Surely no one else had my name, spelt exactly the same? And then I put two and two together. Just before we left Wales, we

....
[9] A Geological background for planning and development in the Afon Teifi catchment, by R A Waters, J R Davies, D Wilson and J K Prigmore, p.8.

had been living in a disused furniture factory not far, I now realised, from this sleepy mid-Teifi town. Derw Mill. We lived in our horsebox outside in the yard, whilst our friends, Chris and Donna, inhabited the top floor of the vast old mill. Up there was a space called The Big Room, and above that a witch apparently lived in the attic.

I only have a handful of memories from that time. I started school in Saron and was an obvious outsider – asking for vegetarian food and soya milk at lunch times, and getting told off for not singing in Welsh during assembly. On my first day I cried inconsolably in the Headmaster's office. Aged five, I had never spent a day away from my parents. Back at the mill I remember playing with my Captain Scarlet figure, and one day I told my mum off for giving me a haircut which, I said, made me resemble Bart Simpson. She burst out laughing. I'd never watched TV.

But my strongest memories from those times are river memories, spent by Afon Seidi, which runs past the mill to join the Teifi at Pentrecwrt. I remember cooking beans over a small fire on a bend of the stream with my dad. I remember Chris showing me the home of a tiny fairy who lived in the bank. I saw her working a loom in a miniature room. And then there was the day that my dad made my mum appear out of thin air. We were walking along the stream when my dad asked me to make a wish. I wished for mum to join us on the walk. She appeared in amongst the ferns by the edge of the path, one welly on, and one welly still in her hands. 'That's strange,' she said, 'I was just putting my wellies on to come and find you both, and now I'm here, as if by magic.'

I pull into the carpark of the old mill. Twenty-five years. The things that happen in a life, in a web of lives, in twenty-five years. Under pressure and forces, the bedrock and the courses of our lives ripple and alter and time moves; nothing stands still, or so it seems.

Years ago, when I was studying philosophy, I came across an unnerving concept about time: eternalism shuns the classical temporal model which categorises time into the three distinct regions of past, present and future. In this latter, common-sense view, the present is the only real moment, and as it moves forward it leaves behind an empty, non-existent past and approaches an unreal future. Eternalism, on the other hand, holds that all existence in time is somehow equally real. This uncanny school of thought tells us that time is not like a river, but more like the laminated strata of rock on a cliff face: layer upon layer of coexistent moments. From this perspective, I never left this strange old mill; and Afon Seidi, which trickles by me now, holds and channels all the waters of her life at once.

I climb a hill and stare at the serene valley of rough pasture winding away into Carmarthenshire, bathed in the russet light of November. The bracken and the oak and the larch have all turned golden. The beeches are ablaze.

I look for the old bank where the fairy had her home, and instead stumble upon a spring hidden in brambles. Water is singing here, inundating the bright grass, shivering, humming downwards, falling as much as it can in its endless pursuit of depth. I've found both magic and miracle, then, of the purest kind. And what time does water know? Nothing beyond its own melodic running; nothing beyond the joy of conjoining and the bliss of movement.

Time isn't what the philosophers tell us, with their logic, or the scientists, with their equations – time isn't even the ticking of clocks. Time is the river's singing; time is the heliotrope's steady turning; time is the autumnal burning of the canopies; time is the carcass of the pigeon lying in the Seidi's ice-clear shallows.

And deep time too surrounds us and is physically visible. When we look at an oak, we don't see the present moment only – we are viewing 250 years of time, right there before our eyes: the time of acorn, root, sap and sun-searching branch; all are written in the present tree's being. When we look at a small crystal brook and the hills that cup it, we are beholding thousands of years of time's slow work – the abrasion of vast glaciers; the weathering of countless, forgotten storms; the erosion down into bedrock of ceaseless cycles of wind and rain; the tide of plant-life and animal-life which laps the land and layers it with loam. The past is preserved, underpinned, present, in the here-and-now.

Perhaps time isn't a thing in itself, then, but rather our own subjective perception of change, of movement, embodied. If we were to pause all atoms and all energy, completely, would time still exist? Imagine a stream that stood truly still – would it not be as if time itself had halted? But what good are thought experiments? They can teach us about our own skill at inventing ideas, but about rivers... time... life? Just dip your fingers slowly into Seidi's currents, and you can know these three things at once.

HOME

....

Rumour has it that I have my origins in this old cottage, Glandwr-isaf. Regardless of the site of my biological beginnings, my soul, like all the trees and plants in this quiet valley, has wound and anchored its roots down into the soil of this place; has fed on and grown from the essence and meanings of this humble building and its situation at the bottom of a lane so steep that these days the rest of the world, it seems, avoids this route. A stone's throw away over a tussocky field, the young Ceri gurgles in a narrow channel, marking the thalweg of the ever-widening valley of sleepy pasture, small woods and sparse, secret farms.

The Cottage. These two generic words have for me always encapsulated a very specific set of feelings, memories and images, which radiate out beyond the whitewashed walls of the building to encompass a landscape for miles around. Approaching it in the car as a child on holiday, landmarks, at first infrequent, steadily increased in number to signal with excitement the rapidly closing gap between "us" and our destination. After hours on the motorway, passing Carmarthen and entering the thickly-wooded slopes of the Gwili's snaking valley marked the journey's first real milestone. This valley was an entrance in a wall of hills that guarded the wild Welsh interior. The body and mind prepared themselves for what lay ahead: stepping out into the fresh, damp air, and listening to the sudden, deep silence that followed the switching off of the hot, tired engine; sleepily and reluctantly helping to unpack the car, opening the old gate with its strange latch and carefully walking up the track, trying to remember where the muddy puddles had formed; the fumbling for keys; the smell of coal in the porch; the fusty, damp air of the living room, and that other smell – the combined aromas of everyone and everything that has inhabited and formed and passed through these walls; the immediate lighting of the open fire, with its simple hearth and mantle of red brick. Such a simple hole in the wall, such profound flames, always the same, that warm our feet and hands and hearts.

It was on the bridge – which really is just a lane traversing an inconvenience – that I first played Poohsticks. I had no name for the stream then. Who could have foreseen that this – the Ceri – would one day wind its way back into my world as a thought tributary in a series of musings about one of Wales's longest rivers? Then, it was just a transparent, flowing creature that carried sticks out of sight and returned them – most of the time – seconds later, on the other side of the tunnel. A basic lesson in cause and effect, and in a world beyond ourselves: actions have consequences; even when things appear to vanish, the world is still dealing with them, moving them on, sensing their ripples; and objects have a life even when we can no longer sense them.

The silence of this place is immense. During the day, of course, there are sounds: the sheep, the birds, the cow on the hill, the faint running of the stream – a "cold tinkle like a spoon on the rim of a cup"[10]; the cry of a buzzard; the bark of a dog; the distant hum of some machine working lazily at a job in a farmyard or field. But even then, these sounds are quiet compared to the silence and the peace which predominate here, and enter one's bones and slow one down, calming the hectic mind from a tumult of habitual thought-waves to the mill-pond stillness of a consciousness reflecting its secluded environment.

At night all sounds – save for the murmuring Ceri and the lonely owl – seem to fade away completely, and one is left alone on the dew-damp grass outside, with nothing but the stars aligned with the hidden valley, the smell of the wet fields, the smoke of the sacred fire (whose light flickers on the face of one's lover, whose body is on the sofa, and whose soul has entered another realm, through a book's portal of words), and one's own wonderment at ending up here, like this, a person in a peaceful place, a soul in silent space, at home.

---

[10] Wil Ifan, *Where I Belong* (Cardiff: Western Mail & Echo Ltd., 1946), p.8.

APRIL: GILLO-FACH

....

To stroll through a vast field in the moist dusk of April, rain waiting in the slow, low sky, birds chattering in woods bursting into moss-green and pale gold and wild cherry white. Crowds of cuckooflowers quivering in crops of lush grass, hovering in constellations on their tall stems. I stand by a cathedral of an oak, its great arms raised to the heavens, its fingers unfurling a thousand new prayers of green. Stout nettles congregate at its feet. In a rain-filled depression nearby, tadpoles journey in all directions: a Brownian motion of wriggling tails; life, pulsing in a puddle.

And when the rain begins to fall softly and the light fades swiftly, I reach the river's edge. A darkness, giving away no secrets. A seeming belt of blackness in a land vernal and fecund. I turn to cross the great field, grateful for stopping at the roadside to receive spring's quiet gifts, to know intimately this evening and this season of bliss. Leverets are here, somewhere, snug in a den of crosshatched grass; the wren eggs are warm in their moss-ball nest in the overhang's roots; worms and moles are busy in the old earth beneath my feet; dandelions nod their furry heads in a breeze that rises and falls like a breath.

Our human worlds go on, complex and cryptic; on an April evening, I step out beyond these things and feel good.

TRIBUTARY: HIRWAUN

In the summer I forget who I am. The busyness, and the business, drown out my real voice, and the voice that says "make more bread, make hay while the sun shines" grows louder in my ear. But sometimes in a moment of clarity, of silence, I am reminded of the world beyond the bakery, and of a sun whose rays and long days should be utilised for nothing more than pure pleasure, and of the real hay bales that lie like pieces of sliced baguette, drying out in the vast fields under the August sky.

the stubble fields
that belong
to the evening sky

In the heat of the bakery, in the middle of lunch service, I decide that I will spend the night by a beloved stream, light a fire, and sleep in my hammock.

the glades, by streams,
where deer make
their paths

The thought of just setting off with a backpack for the night unnerves me a little, but I commit to it – it's happening: I have gone too long without drinking deeply of the wild.

It's a gorgeous, empty valley, over-brimming with woods, cradling soft meadows, profoundly peaceful, cupping the sweet Hirwaun that falls over itself on its way to the Teifi. I spy blackberries and pop a few choice orbs into my mouth: the taste of late summer, the taste of this valley. Magic.

I call in at Pen-ddôl – a ruined croft hidden in woodland beside a field deep in the valley. Sunglow from the west lights up its ivy-clad walls. Odd shaped, rounded stones bulge precariously out from among the squarer slates – these are river boulders, carried across the field, up the gentle slope, from the Hirwaun. They glow with warm light, weighted in their original position, and so bridge that strangeness called time to the hands that placed them here so skilfully, so carefully, so many years ago. Perhaps these small boulders once smouldered with red algae, as so many of the Hirwaun's submerged stones do today. Outside its crumbling walls, facing the door, a huge flat stone like a table sits wedged between trees. Its impeccably level surface is scarred by hundreds of tiny cut marks. I place a rounded river pebble, that I myself have stolen from the Hirwaun, atop this great slab. An offering, left on an altar.

Close by, two ash trees of monumental proportions are in their lushest greenery. These are the guardians of the valley. They stand for its creatures and its plants and give a form to the wind and a song to the rain, and today lend the hillside some shade. I measure their trunks two metres above ground level: both exactly eighteen feet in circumference. To look up from their bases in the sunshine of early evening is to fill one's eyes with copious shades of green; is to witness a twisting shoal of green fish-forms flashing in the honeyed light of a lagoon. Ancient siblings, seventy metres apart; slow, green giants, tree creepers excavating their cracked, creased hides.

Each of the trips in this book, I suppose, represents a small victory over that part of me that is, as the saying goes, "waiting to start to live" (the part that manically organises and plans and saves and orders and waits for "greener grass"; that tries to settle all those affairs that we like to believe will form the groundwork for our dream, for the life we were meant to lead, the basis for our ultimate self). But my wisest self knows that there is no experience more enlivening – more reverential of the raw, pulsating present – than simply immersing oneself quietly in nature. In this quiet place, all ideas of being better, happier, wealthier – even wiser – fall away. For me, this is the dream, this is the ultimate life (a life, after all, is lived in moments): to witness with an open heart and mind the miraculous beauty and harmony of growing things, flowing things, glowing things.

the trembling plants here,
the wild stream,
the rising moon.

To reflect on the strangeness of being in a tranquil valley at dusk, staring at the way the universe arranges itself, organically tangled and all bound up and layered in a series of events that constitute landscape, nature – that shrinking part of the world which bursts through our human constructs and constructions. In this state of awe, it seems miraculous that a stream should flow. How is it possible that a clear fluid can tumble over itself so seamlessly, atop a bed of mud and stones? How – why – is it that such a beautiful thing exists? What does it mean to write about such things? I have no idea.

I'm not alone in my ontological bafflement. Nan Shepherd, too, understood something of water's propensity, through merely flowing forth, to spiritually stupefy: "Like all profound mysteries, it is so simple that it frightens me... It slips out of holes in the earth like the ancient snake. I have seen its birth; and the more I gaze at that sure and unremitting surge of water at the very top of the mountain, the more I am baffled. We make it all so easy, any child in school can understand it... But I don't understand it. I cannot fathom its power." [11]

I came here last in June, and rejoiced then too at life, thriving; at the universe here, dancing in such divine forms:

Sweet the air in June, in the Hirwaun's hidden valley;
Sweet the dreams of the young stag,
Who beds down beneath cloud haze,
Crosshatching and scenting the grass.
Sweet the swaying of water-crowfoot
Beneath a train of vortices;
Sweet the bumble bee taking its fill
From the cups of tufted vetch;
Sweet the brown trout that darts in the shadows;
Sweet the jasmine scent of the bone-cluster spraint,
Smeared on a boulder;
Sweet the small singing from the tree-hole nest of the wren.

[11] Nan Shepherd, *The Living Mountain* (Edinburgh: Canongate Books, 2011), pp.23 and 27.

Before I strike the match, I breathe in the dusk, and stare up at the dappled canopy. Squinting, the small patches of pale sky between dark leaves become like clustering stars. I listen to the stream's singing: I am wild water, miracle of the old earth, and I come running through the quiet dusk to bring joy to the world.

I strike the match, and now a crackling joins the stream's singing, and it says: I am fire, miracle of the stars, and I come blazing through lonely space to bring you warmth and company tonight.

After a supper of stew and bread, I rekindle the fire and gaze into the hungry flames that ward off the total night about me. Try as I might, I can't seem to fully relax. I have become a wild animal again, on guard – there are no walls now between my small self and the wide world.

An owl comes, screeching and circling just beyond the reach of the fire's light, shouting to the night about the strange beast that flickers bright on the riverbank.

I keep half-expecting to look up from this page to find a fox sat across from me, its eyes ablaze with hypnotic flames. I climb into my hammock and drift off to the chattering of the Hirwaun's thousand voices.

all night,
inhaling what the wood exhales:
such a pure air

the dawn chorus
spreading through the woods
of Britain
like wild fire

MAP

....

Nature is a messy and recalcitrant thing. Of course, in and of itself it's perfect – just as it should be; but bring human preferences and priorities into its equation, and its relative chaos and absolute disregard for our designs and projects is clear.

Today, for example, on my map I spotted a footpath leading through fields along the Arberth, a tributary that feeds the Teifi at Llechryd. On the map the theoretical journey appeared straightforward, literally. According to its symbols, and to my own preconceptions, progress would be granted unimpeded: the green line dotted neatly across pure white suggested as much – or rather, my naïve, sub-conscious interpretation of this tiny, symbolic thoroughfare led me to believe in the myth of "ideal movement": ideal in the sense of what I wanted – of what would be ideal – and also in the sense of movement that is theoretical, mental, that forgets the reality of an actual body moving through particular, nuanced space.

It takes two to tango: on the one hand, the human who perpetually forgets just how big the gap is between the signifier and the signified, the word and the world, the sign and the site; on the other, the deceptive, seductive reduction of the map which – in its trick of scale and spatial categorisation – wants us to believe that this gap is small. Maps, of course, are our own invention, but just because they aid us, that's not to say they can't deceive us in equal measure.

I drive out of town and head to a bridge in the hills where I park my car. I hop a fence and stand staring at the field. I had collaborated with my map in order to forget that a tiny, flat, white square on paper can signify what in reality is a giant, sloping, water-logged mess, half grass, half mud. I return to my car and put on some slightly more water-proof shoes.

I head up the hill with the aim of traversing a narrower spring. It almost works: the spring, although significantly smaller than the bog at the bottom of the hill, is just a little too wide to hop. My boots become soggy. Already, then, I have strayed from the planned route: whilst the map pulls me one way, promising linear progress, nature forces me to and fro, writing weird shapes with me – glyphs in the muddy grass – as I try to navigate the language of a living terrain.

Maps (especially paper ones) are implicitly historical

entities – out-dated, one-dimensional. Nature, by contrast, rides the wave of the present – is, in fact, the very crest of time itself. Even in its small, seasonal flooding of a single field, nature asserts its rule.

But the limitations of maps can offer surprises as well as frustrations. Having zig-zagged up the hill and back down, I spy the Arberth emerging from a wooded knoll. As I get closer, it becomes apparent that the knoll conceals a steep-sided gorge. My god – the things that exist just off the main road, just off the beaten track, in our endless, forgotten fields. The muddy little stream pours forth from the ravine, and I stand watching from the quarried crags above. The slopes are tangled with bramble, carpeted with ferns – there's no way down. This unexpected gorge is simply too steep and short-lived to be represented by contour lines on the map.

Through the trees, high above on the opposite bank, I glimpse a house. I had seen a small square on the map earlier, but being nameless (a rarity in Wales, land of language, with a language of land), I had presumed it a ruin. The thought that someone inhabits it is a disappointing one, here in what I thought was an empty valley. I wander on, hoping to survey it from another angle. I pass a polypore, as old as the ore of the oak on which it feeds, from which it shelves its many selves, and bleeds. A beefsteak fungus. No map can capture the emergence of fungi – overnight or over the slow course of the years – nor the spores that float through the wood and out over the twilight fields.

As I skirt the edge of the gorge, I glance at the field off to my right. Through it – a tiny, temporary torrent – water flows, a ribbon of sky in the fold of the hillside; a silver serpent slithering through grass, barely a foot wide. I ascend to the height of the adjacent house, still masked by trees. This was one hill once, before the river carved it in half. Down below, upstream, the Arberth is free from the gorge. Being high up, this vantage point gives the impression that the river is flowing up and over a hump. Away to my right, an undulating expanse of ploughed field. The pterodactyl silhouette of a heron flaps slowly toward a bloom of bruised cloud, which itself moves to smother the smudge of chalk in the sky's haze – a waxing, gibbous moon.

A line of cows advances towards me, unknowingly, beyond an arm of trees which cluster a slope. They'll be my barrier today. This, after all, is their land: a place to ruminate and squelch through mud, beneath cloud and moon. On my way back through the fields, I too ruminate and squelch through mud, and walk a straight line, through inundated grass. Nothing now can be ruined by wet shoes – the walk is done, the enchantment has been harvested from these bare fields, studded with distant oaks and cows, sliced through and blessed by the Arberth.

In early 2015 I moved from Llandysul to Cardigan to open Bara Menyn Bakehouse & Café, thus greatly limiting the time available to me for exploring the Teifi. In the depths of winter especially – when the light drained quickly from the day just as I was cleaning down and cashing up – finding time to walk became a depressing challenge.

One evening I laid out my maps in the living room, planning to search out new walks: if I couldn't walk now, I would walk later, armed with fresh ideas. But as well as highlighting new potential routes, I also ended up revisiting old haunts. In this way, in my flat above the bakery – with the wind and rain howling outside in the 5pm dark – I took to re-walking the river via the map. By translating this two-dimensional world back to its real-world counterpart, I was reacquainting myself with my old friend. Only, this imaginative translation was partial, like a fractured, flickering screen. Beyond the reduced and the remembered, on the periphery of memory, darkness lay. The facts of the map and the magic of the mind could only collaborate so far. But it was good enough for me: it was a promise, a power, a portable panorama.

Before long I took to revisiting my childhood haunts of Dartmoor and the South Hams in map form, and realised just how small my world had once been. Today, most of Ceredigion feels homely to me – that is, I somehow feel permitted to explore and to familiarise myself with a much vaster territory. Perhaps the sparse population can in part account for this. In rural places we have to form broader communities. As a teenager, anything beyond the hills surrounding the town I lived in verged on the alien.

At the time my connection to the landscape was lived single-mindedly, innocently, on ground level; following my nose, my instinct. Maps were not consulted. Somehow back then there was no need for them. What is it these days that so intrigues me about maps – about having the living landscape reconfigured through symbol and geometry to these lifeless representations smoothed out before me on the floor? It is partly because they are not in fact lifeless: our imagination impregnates these inky, crinkled terrains with meaning, memory and movement. It's about accessibility and breadth of comprehension too: we become like birds or gods, surveying vast vistas, perceiving panoramas invisible to the map-less pedestrian. We stitch together points and places into lines and webs of belonging and becoming. On our maps we beat bounds both with our eyes and our hearts, and plant new seeds of land-longing.

Now, looking back, I see how that wood linked to that lane; my friend's house to the source of that nameless tributary; I see how two places are in fact close though I'd believed them to be far apart. Maps contain dictionaries too, in the old poems and songs scattered across their paper landscapes of topographic similes.

In the dim light of this small room in the old custom house of Cardigan, I learn the curious names of those streams and brooks by which my child self played, and my adolescent self lost himself, sought himself and found pieces of himself in the crystal waters of those Dartmoor streams: River Mardle (which shares its name with my first primary school teacher; I buried treasure near the source of this stream at Chalk Ford for my little brother);

Holy Brook (I built a miniature house made from river stones on a beach-bend of this one); Dean Brook (where at Cross Furzes I wrote my first poem, 'Off the beaten track...'); and then that nameless stream that cuts down through King's Wood, where, on a small island, I found a ground nest full to the brim with fresh, freckled eggs, the sight of which astounded me, and haunts me with its beauty to this day.

On the Dart itself, downstream of Badger's Holt, I spent my first night alone in the wild, aged seventeen. Here I wrote a poem which means a great deal to me, and even now transports me back to that solitary, summer evening high on the moors:

What is it
In the dancing smoke
And crackling fire
That makes man's life
Seem pure again?
What is it
In the greenness, reflected
On the sliding stillness
Of the river's surface?
In the shifting skies?
In the birdsong heard
In the crepuscular hour,
In the freshness
After heavy rain?

When man
Swims naked
In the evening pools –
Alone,
But not too far away –
Why is he moved
By a force that pleases
And calms his hectic soul?
From a life
Full of noise
– inner and outer –
Why does he choose
To step into the quiet?

Here the boundaries
Crumble and dissolve.
There is no pretending
Anymore.
The deer on the river island;
The squirrel within reach;
The soaring buzzard in the sky;
The wild horses,
Jumping fish;
The ancient stone,
And scent of ferns;
The dome of heaven above.

CATCH

....

"I in these flowry Meads wo'd be:
These Christal streams should solace me;
To whose harmonious bubling noise,
I with my Angle wo'd rejoice..." [12]

Nearly three years into my love affair with the Teifi, a desire grew in me to poach new treasures from her depths. I had spent so many hours trespassing nervously, searching fruitlessly, moving along her length aimlessly, thinking obscurely; now it was time to be still, to be empty, to find, to be focussed, to inhabit the river legally: the time had come to learn to fish.

After months of idling and wondering where to begin, a chance arose to get to grips with the basics when I spent a week alone on Ynys Enlli, with little to do but walk, read, write and – thanks to a friend who was rightly sceptical of

12 Izaak Walton, 'The Angler's Wish', from *The Compleat Angler* (1653).

my ability to be a true hermit and thus suggested I borrow his rod – learn to fish. So I taught myself to tie a blood knot, arrange floats, weights and hooks in the correct order, and finally to cast the whole lot out into the cold, grey sea.

I caught nothing on that lonely trip – it was the ocean that stole things from me, clinging with a vice-like grip on to my ill-cast rig with its seaweed hands. But I – if not the fish – had become hooked; watching the steady trajectory of the tackle looping through the air seemed akin to a breath-watching meditation; a lesson in Zen was intimated: in seeking something, nothing was found.

I returned home with the confidence to seek out a quiet riverbank and interact with my multifaceted friend in a new and infinitely exciting way. But the journey would be long, and not all of it would be pleasant.

The first fish I brought home was not one I'd caught myself. I had been spinning for sewin in the mild, July twilight, without any luck, when a man approached the bank and set up his gear a few metres away over the reeds. He cast out his worm and weight, accompanied by a small, green LED light. Within minutes he had something on his line and came over to my patch to land it. He reeled it in through the dark water and lifted it out into the gloom. 'What is it?' 'A flatfish.' I had no idea that flatfish even lived in freshwater rivers such as the Teifi. 'Is "flatfish" actually its proper name?' I asked. He looked at me suspiciously. 'Yes,' he replied. 'Can you eat them?' I asked. 'Can do,' he said, 'but I'll put him back in. Unless you want it?' The thought of returning home with a fish seemed better than the alternative. 'Ok, if that's alright?' I answered. 'I'll cook it up.' He bagged it up and then handed it to me. I placed the plastic bag down behind me and continued to hunt for something more appealing – casting out in anticipation of a bite. Something rustled on the ground behind me. The black bag was moving. I turned round and called across to my companion: 'Are you sure it's dead? It's twitching... Rigor mortis is it?' 'Just nerves,' he said, matter-of-factly.

Ten minutes later, when it was so dark that I could no longer see, and having got my hook caught up in reeds twice in less than two minutes, I packed up, thanked him, and drove home. Halfway back, the bag rustled and shook on the seat beside me. 'Surely it's not dead,' I thought to myself. As I neared the bridge, I imagined myself throwing it back into the water. 'But it must be dead,' I told myself, 'he said it was dead. Muscle spasms must go on for ages in fish.'

When I got back to the bakery, I slid the dark, slippery muscle out into a plastic container. 'Fuck. It's still breathing.' I got a larger tub, filled it under the cold tap, and re-housed the sad-looking creature in a deeper pool of water, although there was still no room for it to turn around, let alone to swim. I placed it on the stainless-steel workbench under the bright kitchen lights, and stared at it, wondering what to do. Half an hour or so before this fish had been feeding on the muddy bed of the Teifi – had been so much more a part of the Teifi than I would ever be – and now it was trapped in a small bowl, having drowned in waterless air for close to forty minutes, its gills opening and closing rhythmically, bits of bloody globules floating in the water around it, a hook barbed somewhere in its small mouth. It had the appearance of an alien, with eyes staring upward from the top of its head. 'I should hit it on the head with a rolling pin,' I argued to myself, 'and the chef can cook it up tomorrow and we can see what "flatfish" tastes like. I decided to bring it home, and now I have to deal with it; I have to respect its life by killing it; by not allowing this suffering – this humiliation – to continue.' I began to look around for the right implement, but quickly gave up. I couldn't do it. I thought about holding it and trying to take the hook out, but I couldn't do that either. 'I'm going to have to take you back to the river,' I said.

And so it was. I walked through town, along the lamp-lit, eleven o'clock streets, through an industrial estate and down a mud-caked slipway to the tidal Teifi. I poured the dark, smelly, half-dead slipper of a thing into the murky shallows, wondering whether a fish from above the weir could survive the salt of the estuary, and then banished such sensible pessimism from my mind. What was the use? The damage had already been done. A spirit, an aqueous agent of the Teifi had been dragged from its element and abused – abused by a lack of compassion (had the fisherman even tried to kill it before giving it to me?), abused by ignorance, curiosity and fear (these latter crimes had been committed by myself alone).

It lay in the inky wash, only its rising gills catching the distant street lights and giving it away. I pushed it out into deeper water, and hoped it would live, and flourish, and survive with a hook in its mouth, even as I doubted those same hopes.

I didn't decide to stop fishing after that curious incident of the fish in the night-time; but I resolved to be a better, kinder, more knowledgeable fisherman.

I found out later that the fish I had dealt with that night had been a flounder, which in the summer, especially at night, will venture from the coast up into estuaries, and even beyond them to full freshwater, to feed. Its name seemed sadly appropriate: on the one hand, "flounder" means to struggle or stagger clumsily in mud or water, which in the end had been its fate as it lay there breathing in the slime of the slipway; on the other hand, it means to show or feel great confusion, which had been what I myself had done when I'd tried to decide whether to put it out of its misery or not. Flounder.

You wait and wait and wait for the first time, knowing that it will, like losing your virginity, be life-changing; and then it happens all of sudden, when you're least expecting it, and the dream becomes a reality; the fantastical fiction becomes another familiar fact: something is fighting and writhing on the end of your line and you think: 'This is it, it's happening. My first fish.'

It happened for me after two months of fruitless fishing, one blue evening at the end of August, full of haze and mist and the smoke of bonfires drifting from distant farms.

I was driving to my usual stretch of river, for which I have a permit, when I decided that I didn't want to go where everyone else was going; that I wanted a new stretch of river to befriend. I stopped my car in a layby beside a huge field bordering the river, and traipsed through dewy, knee-high grass, aware of my imminent status as a poacher. The river was low and straight and idle in the bat-flit, fly-buzz dusk as I waded out into its clear glides and cast my small spinner out into the wide ribbon of rippling sky.

I caught three small brown trout that evening, all in the space of ten minutes – muscular distillations, scaly concentrations, of Teifi. I tried to kill them as quickly as possible to limit their suffering, bashing their heads with river stones, but they kept slipping from my hands and flipping about on the bank, trying in vain to return home.

To take a life from the river – from anywhere or anything – is a grave act, full of meaning and sorrow and questions: who am I to trick such a perfect being – to hook a pebble-speckled spirit with a barb and fling it from water to land, from deep, ancient life to shallow, early death? A being already so precariously perched on the tightrope of survival in the wild. Who am I to step into the river and alter its ecology? Such an ambivalent act: all this guilt and culpability on the one hand; and on the other: the beauty of being ankle-deep in the river, feeling its irresistible tug against your legs, miles from anywhere, the body moving slowly, consciously, enchanted and intoxicated by the dancing elements, the mind focussed, aware of all the small, miraculous happenings of this quiet, self-sustaining water-world: the swift passing of the ducks;

the arrival of the woodpigeon high in the ash; the shivering of the willow in full leaf; the soft undulations of the emerald ranunculus; the sippings of the trout that ripple out in mandalas of light; the joy of having a task, a challenge; the thrill of hunting for Teifi's elusive, sentient jewels; the adrenaline that arrives with the bite and the battle on the end of the line.

And then the moment, itself beyond sorrow and joy – located in primal silence – when the disturbed flame must be extinguished.

Little Sewin, 05/10/16

Little sewin
Plucked from the riffle
Between estuary and gorge
Hawk-still in the wave-wind
Between two worlds
Lifted like a pendant
On a strap of leather
Out into the dusk-chill air
And knocked, with a river stone,
Out of this place,
Where the first starlings murmur
Above the dying reeds
And the last geese circle
Beneath the closed eye of the moon.

Tonight your perfect head
Begins its decay in a bag by my door.
Taking your life so, all I can say is this:
I too will one day be plucked
From this place
Where the birds come and go,
And the river goes on
With its running.

"According to local tradition, each of the eight casts belonging to Cilgerran coracle men had its own characteristics, expressed in a doggerel verse passed down over many generations to the present day:

Bwrw byr hyfryd – Brocen ddryslyd
(Lovely Bwrw byr – complex Brocen)
Gwegrydd lana – Nantyffil lwma
(Cleanest Gwegrydd – poorest Nantyffil)
Crow'n rhoddi – Pwll du'n pallu
([when] Crow gives – Pwlldu refuses)
Bwmbwll yn hela – Draill fach yn dala
(when one hunts at Bwmbwll – you may catch at Draill fach)" [13]

....
[13] J Geraint Jenkins, *Nets and Coracles* (Newton Abbot: David & Charles, 1974), p.143.

A few days later I was unexpectedly invited to a barbeque that the coracle fisherman were putting on to celebrate the end of the netting season. When I arrived at Dolbadau in the gorge below Cilgerran Castle, it was dusk and the beer had obviously been flowing for some time. But as I approached the loose circle gathered around a fire, the laughing lessened a little as most of them stopped to ponder why a stranger had wandered into their midst. Once I'd said hello and sat down, the relaxed atmosphere resumed; and when, having struck up some conversation, a few of them realised that I was the baker from Bara Menyn, and had been born in Ceredigion – that I was a hard-working local just like them, and not merely an English lad writing about an alien land, and river – I was welcomed into the clique as a guest. There were about twenty-five blokes and a couple of women: a motley crew, as I found out later, of electricians, tree surgeons, painter and decorators, canoe instructors, gardeners, builders, shop owners. Listening to their particular banter, I soon realised that the main medium of their conversation was that of witty insult: 'Aled here's a painter – got a nice new set of watercolours, haven't you *bach*?'

Once the light had disappeared completely, it was time to take it in turns to have one last trawl of the season. It was a slow process, a good forty-five-minute round trip to drift down the pitch-black gorge and then to walk back up the riverbank to the car park. A few pairs disappeared into the blackness and returned empty handed. Then it was Dan and Rich's turn. When they approached the circle nearly an hour later, it looked as though they too had been out of luck, but then Dan removed the coracle from his back to reveal what his other hand had been carrying over his shoulder: a beast of a fish. I'd never seen anything like it. There were cheers from the men. It had been a lean few months they said, and what a way to end it. The fish was placed in a baby's bathtub, filling it up and flexing awkwardly to fit in; still twitching a little. Everyone came over for a better view, shining their torches and phones down on to the silvery scales and uttering words of disbelief and admiration. Some said it was a sewin, others that it was unmistakably a salmon. The latter party turned out to be right. Once Dan had quenched his thirst with a jug of beer, it was time for the weighing. Everyone placed their well-educated guesses with a great deal of relish. 'What is it then, Dan?' 'Fifteen and a half pounds,' he said, 'second biggest fish of the season.'

'Fancy a go in a coracle then, Jack?' Dan asked me later on. My immediate reaction was, 'Yes, that would be great.' But as I wandered off to get my wellies, I quickly took stock of the offer: to climb into a notoriously unstable craft for the first time, in a deep, fast-flowing stretch of water, in the pitch-black, guided from the bank by a bunch of drunk fishermen. A sudden uneasiness took hold of me, and an imaginary headline from tomorrow's *Tivyside* scrolled across my mind's eye: 'Local Baker Drowns in Drunken Coracle Escapade'. I left the wellies in my car and walked back to tell Dan that I'd probably fall in, and better leave the lesson for another time – a sober session in the daytime perhaps. He said that I should join them on one of their coracle pub crawls, where they would drift down from Cenarth to St Dog's, stopping at all the Teifi-side watering holes along the way.

I wished I could have stayed down there drinking and talking to the fisherman about their river, but I had to be up early, and so said my thank-yous and farewells, and headed off into the dark – an image of a regal, ancient, monstrous salmon etched on to my retinas. And driving home I wondered what had gone through Dan's mind as he had raised his polished priest to crush the skull of such a fine fish...

By the 17th of October, the season for salmon and sewin has come to an end. Yellowing leaves drift in the torrent like the tattered sails of wrecked ships, and the last of the wrinkled sloes grow a fur of fine mould. The balsam has gone to seed, exploding its offspring at the slightest tremble of the breeze. Little rain has fallen these past few weeks, so the Teifi's waters roll seaward as a liquid lens, magnifying and clarifying the mysterious riverbed world of stone, mud, algae, weed and larvae.

The day before the season's end I pay a visit to my favourite stretch of river, just upstream of Llandysul. It seems that the places we love have the power to cast spells over us: walking into these quiet fields, a peace immediately settles over me. *Lle i enaid gael llonydd* – a place of tranquillity; a place where the soul can know peace. I'm back in my element, my heartland, my *cynefin*.

I wade into the shallow riffles above my island and begin to cast out my tiny trout rapala. Before long, I realise with surprise that I have virtually no desire to catch a fish; just being here, dancing with the river, is enough. Perhaps after months of searching, then, I have gleaned a small pearl of angler-wisdom: finally I have learnt that fishing is mostly about not fishing – rather, its principle joy and truth is to be found through those doors which are opened by the key of entering the water and casting the mind, along with one's line, out and away into the river-world. Now, at last, I believe those tales of anglers who fish with neither bait nor hook; who are simply waiting to be caught by something wiser, other, greater than themselves.

NEST: LLAIN-FFOREST

....

For These

An acre of land between the shore and the hills,
Upon a ledge that shows my kingdoms three,
The lovely visible earth and sky and sea
Where what the curlew needs not, the farmer tills:

A house that shall love me as I love it,
Well-hedged, and honoured by a few ash trees
That linnets, greenfinches, and goldfinches
Shall often visit and make love in and flit:

A garden I need never go beyond,
Broken but neat, whose sunflowers every one
Are fit to be the sign of the Rising Sun:
A spring, a brook's bend, or at least a pond:

For these I ask not, but, neither too late
Nor yet too early, for what men call content,
And also that something may be sent
To be contented with, I ask of Fate. [14]

Edward Thomas

I can see myself making a home here in this secluded valley, where spring arrives early and the noise of the world is kept at bay by the thickly wooded slopes that encircle these Arcadian fields. More than that – I have actually found a home; and even if I cannot live here, which surely I cannot, today I have discovered my home: an old stone cottage, Llain Fforest, with thick walls and no roof, save for two spindly rafters of heart oak, propping each other up in their last years. They will go down together; return to the earth of the woodland from which they grew. The stone too will eventually crumble back into the very ground from which it was chiselled: Llain Fforest sits at the foot of a hill, in an excavated nook, half tucked-away from any foul weather that comes its way.

We could grow old together here in this forgotten *cwm*. Learn the ancient lessons of living and dying, in the green peace of this pasture, with its rushes where snipe sleep, and its secret stream where otters creep, thriving on the flesh of the plump trout that abound in its deep, absinthe pools. We could learn about simplicity

---

[14] Edward Thomas, *Collected Poems* (London: Faber & Faber, 1979), p.101.

and self-sufficiency in this south-facing cottage, with its vast hearth, its nettles nestling by the doorstep where I sit; its daffodils unfurling in an empty field, which was a garden once.

I stand up, stretch in the first heat of the year, and turn into the ruin's coolness. I step slowly toward the hearth, beholding its enormity before ducking slightly and entering it as one would a small room. I reach into a damp hollow at the back of the fireplace, where a stone has been dislodged, and move my fingers carefully through the cold, dark loam of decaying mortar. I find a ceramic lid, a tiny horseshoe and a metal hook. The first I pocket, the other two I hang on giant nails that have been driven between bricks inside the cavernous chimney, which steadily, neatly narrows to a square foot of blueness.

This grand hearth, with its massive mantle of rough-hewn oak, was – is – the heart and soul of the house. Its light and warmth and magic were essential companions for lives that knew darkness and coldness and dullness all too well when it was time to leave its side. Whose faces flickered in the shadows here? Which stories were spoken to the quiet crackling of its fire? What dreams were glimpsed, which memories rekindled, in its flames?

Edward Thomas knew about these old Welsh firesides and the visions they could induce: "We became as the logs, that now and then settled down (as if they wished to be comfortable) and sent out, as we did words, some bristling sparks of satisfaction... As we kneeled, and our sight grew pleasantly dim, were we looking at fireborn recollections of our own childhood, or at a golden age that never was?"[15]

The neighbouring house of Felin-ganol Isaf on the other side of the valley – a hundred years behind this one on its journey to ruin – bulges precariously like a squat mushroom in the damp woods, readying to explode its histories and ghosts to the wind like spores; impatient to expose the last of its homely contents to forces that will erase them indelibly. Strange meanings, trapped in objects, will dissolve back into the mud. The meaning of the ceramic barn owl that sits on the dining table, staring through a window; of the mouldy image of Christ, hand outstretched, who gazes at the fireplace; of the menagerie of brass animals on the windowsill – duck-billed platypus, unicorn, owl, kangaroo, wallaby, cockatoo, lizard, koala, and a railway carriage that says "San Francisco" on it.

And then the Red Cross Certificate by the front door, awarded to a Miss Rowena Bowen of Bronwilfa, in 1913 – now a home for woodworm that munch their tunnels up against the glass, slowly erasing the ornate borders, heading hungrily for the dates and names at the centre.

---

[15] Edward Thomas, *Wales* (Oxford: Oxford University Press, 1983), p.47.

Wandering home in the dusk through the ancient farmyard of Penralltddu, I bump into Valmai James, who was born in this valley, just a few fields away. She farmed Penralltddu alone for fifteen years between 1960 and 1975, growing corn and cutting hay in the meadows and caring for her cows – just one petite, rosy-cheeked woman working a whole farm. She says that 'the old ones would be happy to know that people are taking an interest in this valley and its ruins.' She knew the inhabitants of Felin Ganol Isaf and Llain Fforest, who eventually moved away to Swansea for a less toilsome life.

Sometimes, pondering a question, she slips into a reverie, and leans on her stick as she bows low, as if the ground itself has memories to share. Valmai is of this land, just as the burr oaks above Llain Fforest are, hosting this valley's creatures, growing old in the rising tide of spring's green sea. So Valmai is host to this valley's people and past, so many seasons and years, so many births and deaths layered like the dark loam and the new life which grows from it. Valmai is a very old Welsh word for mayflower, and it suits this lady well: sprightly, glowing, with a twinkle in her eye. 'It's good to be out on such evenings,' she says, 'now the days are getting longer.' 'It is,' I say, 'there's hope in the air now.' I say farewell, and tell her I'll bring her a Welsh loaf next time I'm passing – wheat from Trelech, sea salt from Ynys Môn and spring water from Brynberian – a taste of our land, for someone who knows it so well; a taste of the olden days, for someone who knew them so well.

I return to the Piliau valley a month later, entering into its secret fields through a glacial gorge below Pen-y-bryn, and wandering upstream in the shadows of early evening. In its dark, damp heart, I come to an ancient mill, Gaer Woollen Factory, once fed by a leat chiselled into the hillside. Upstream, where the leat sneaks away from the Piliau, the river has been slowed and pooled by a great sloping weir-like wall to create a kind of millpond. Here, beside the white water that spits off the ancient stonework, a pair of dippers have built their moss-ball nest. From below, it sits just out of reach of the Piliau's greedy hands; and from above, just out of reach of hungry foxes. A balancing act in all senses of the phrase, and a beautiful one. I hide in the leat behind a huge ash and wait for the parents to return with food. Somewhere in that deep green ball that blurs into the moss of the bank, a brood of tiny dippers are waiting too. What a place to build a hanging home, by the Piliau's ceaseless roar in a forgotten valley which once buzzed with industry: quarries, mills, farms, kilns, even forts and castles. Rivers and valleys and the hills around them were once indispensable for the energy and passage and defence they provided. This century, it seems, has no need for such things – we have abstract electric, and machines that build roads wherever they're needed, and no need for castles. And so these places lie quiet, crumbling, reclaimed by nature, on the periphery of modern con-sciousness, barely remembered, visited even less.

Strange then that this place should be at the centre of my consciousness and visited by me often – then again, I can think of nothing more useful than spying on dippers in the dusk, and imagining the warmth of their perfect nest, and the primal hunger of their chicks, which have yet to venture out into this strange, dangerous world, and search for a waterfall and a home of their own.

I would raise chicks on the Piliau's banks, in the nest of Llain Fforest, and move, somehow, closer to the world of the valley's birds and beasts, trees and shifting skies; closer to its toil and its soil, and closer to the small gods that dwell here in the green and the quiet.

TRIBUTARY: PILIAU

I hitch a lift out of town to a place where a stream passes under a road. It has often beckoned me whilst I hurtle by in my car; asked me to trace its course; this stream that rises near a crossroads in Pembrokeshire and flows on to cling on to an enclave of Ceredigion on the south side of the Teifi.

I creep into the garden of Rhygwyn, unsure now if the house is empty. There's a sack of sand at the foot of the door. The Piliau, like a thief in the night, must crawl over the lip of the bank which erodes the small garden and try to creep in, seeking treasures to add to its hoard of detritus.

But today I am the thief – I have come to reclaim a portion of these human relics from the wild river. Today the stream is my road, and I have become, in a way, like a deer or an otter or a dipper. I have entered the overlooked waterway – a groove between two planes, a boundary between two counties, a non-place, twisting and turning and eating the earth, singing its own clear song of birth and decay.

A toppled, mossy trunk has become a bridge from a shingle beach to the higher bank; like the otter who scurries here, I too make use of it, and examine the dark ooze of spraint as I pass. Like the deer who's left a pale tuft of hair on this barb of wire, I too hop the fence from the cultivated field of civilisation to this vestige of untamed space which is crammed on the banks of this recalcitrant brook, that bustles and meanders its way through a human-gridded landscape.

But unlike the true inhabitants of this world, I am alive to something they do not see, cannot understand. Just as I cannot read the current – do not even see its words; just as I cannot hear the voices in the wind or see the scent-scenes it carries – so they are blind to the meaning and value I find amongst the river stones.

I become, then, half man, half beast, as I scavenge on the Piliau's pottery shards – pieces of a human world, stolen, broken, discarded, swept under the watery carpet that laps at the back of the garden.

Like a moth lusting after neon, or a badger rootling for bulbs, I am drawn on downstream to each new beach-bend, hungry for the drug of treasure which I instinctively define as those objects of rarity, beauty and meaning.

Out here in this parochial wilderness – this unfrequented kilometre of farmland stream bordered by narrow strips of trees – I become again a child and remember how to play. My mindset is like that of an animal – single-minded, present, searching, moving on. This is the antithesis of work – this "useless journey"; this is play, is art; is the most useful thing of all.

This is an ecstatic manner of inhabiting the world. There is nothing to do but move and feast on this crust of miraculous activity. Who can say whence this stream emerges? Whence this pinky glow through dusk rain shines? Whence this flying shape – that is a wood pigeon returning in the gloom – took flight? Who can say how this opening behind the eyes – like a star, like a black hole – is connected to these things? Who cares?

In these hours of play after work I become beast and feast on the glorious uselessness, on the inherent value, of the infinite mother – Mother Nature.

But now as I sit on a trunk of willow, staring into gloaming fields, the stream too grows dark; and as I stand to leave, my bag feels heavy with pottery. In the distance the lights of the town twinkle. It's time to harbour a purpose again, to find a human path (a dry boardwalk above the tangled chaos of the marsh) and head homeward, trying not to slip in the dark. I smell woodsmoke, and desiring warmth I draw my coat about me. It's time to remember I'm no longer a beast; time to think again, and feel hunger for human needs; to be alert in the black copse tunnel, where in the dusk the daffodils of St David's Day are as dark as the mud from which they quiver forth; to be grateful for the lamplight of the bypass, to crave a hot shower to wash away the river-smell that clings to my skin like a mould.

I am not wild – I only play at being so. I am nothing like those animals I felt an affinity with two hours ago. Even in their hidden streams I seek out signs of my own kind, shards of my own self. The gate of the nature reserve clicks shut behind me. I have come from the river to the town.

JUNE IN THE PILIAU VALLEY

Strong winds shake new leaves to the ground, heavy rain washes shards of slate on to the old track that winds its way down through the woods of the glacial ravine, where a nameless tributary of the Piliau trickles. Rotten branches have been culled from the canopy. Clouds trundle by overhead, interspersed with low sunburst from the west. With the disappearance of spring's prim vigour, scruffy summer makes its entrance into the vale. Sparse elder is in full and gorgeous bloom at the edge of these hidden meadows. Honeysuckle, long in leaf, threatens to unfurl its clenched, green fists into elegant hands and send the whole wood into a perfumed reverie. But for now, it's the bitter musk of fox that scents the air. Save for the odd campion disturbing shady regions with its pink glare, these woods are absent of flowers now.

Felin Ganol Isaf looks more encroached upon than ever – an ash has taken root where the roof has collapsed. The days of this old croft are numbered, and numbered low.

In the stream, tassels of water dropwort, so uptight and turgid yesterday, now resemble ranunculus plants as they lie flattened and swaying in the water. Drier neighbours host their first white umbels. I find a piece of egg-shaped quartz. How long, I wonder – for how many millennia – has the Piliau been sculpting this white stone, so smooth and snug now in my palm?

Returning through the woods in the dusk, two tawny owl fledglings startle from their perch and swoop low over my head. In the high fields again, the sky is ablaze before me; behind me, the cold white waxing of the moon high in blueness.

After a long, hard week at Bara Menyn, all I really want to do is get a takeaway, watch a film and have a long, deep sleep in a king-size bed all to myself whilst Seren is away. So why, then, on a night the rains are coming, do I pack my bivvy bag, some matches and some bread, and head out into the twilight of the Piliau valley? Only a small part of me desired the wild tonight – but somehow this part has won (this part that argues: 'You only live once! Learn something new! Feel something fresh!'). So here I am, traipsing through the darkening wood, in the ominous air, leaving the gentle, sporadic susurration of the road behind, to seek out a nest for the night, to shelter from the storm, to kindle a hopeful fire, and be close to the old earth.

The wind is beginning to caress the leafy trees, making

them dance slowly to the evening's birdsong. I step out from the woods into the valley – a temple of green, honouring the green gods. Steep oak forests as soft and rich as moss. Before setting up camp, I retrieve my camera trap which has been trained on the Piliau for three days now.

Where to bed down? I scurry about like a rodent or dog, sensing the suitability of surface and site, unsatisfied, seeking unknown criteria that must somehow amount to an ideal situation.

Nowhere seems to do: too dark, too damp, too steep, too close to a field full of cows. Instinctively I climb higher, out of the woods, and reach a secluded meadow with a wide view of the valley. I build a basic structure from fallen branches and cover it with a tarp. Now I see – it was light and space and sight I needed.

In a soft shower I manage to light a fire. Woodsmoke in a wild Welsh valley – made for each other like bread and butter.

As I lie in my bed watching the embers' glow fade in the rain, it occurs to me that, in a round-about way, my original plans and desires for a takeaway, a film and a big bed all to myself have been fulfilled to a far greater extent than anything I had envisaged earlier on: I "takeaway" homemade pittas from the bakery and toast them over the fire; and for dessert, snug in my shelter, I open a small box of my friend's herbal chocolates and pop each delicious sphere into my mouth with a joy enhanced by the drizzly dusk; for a film, once inside my sleeping bag, I check the footage on my camera trap and watch in amazement as a heron stalks the shallows before pouncing out of shot on its unsuspecting prey. To be able to move toward Piliau trout without them noticing – a god-like, impossible feat. And as for a king-size bed, well... my bed tonight is giant-size – a whole meadow on which to lay my head, under the pitter-patter music of the rain on the tarpaulin.

It's a full moon tonight, but I doubt it'll show its face – it's too wet and cloudy to be up and about on such a night. Only the sheep and the cattle and the horses and the wilder creatures are out right now – and me, remembering my wild side, reacquainting myself with the wind and the rain and the grass and the night-time noises, and honouring the green gods of the Piliau's paradise pastures.

SPIRIT

....

I step out on to St. Mary Street. A zephyr hurries by, bringing with it warm scents of sun-baked stone and mown grass. A heady perfume of flowers has also found its way down this old street, where a man with a guitar passes. I sit on my slate-stoned doorstep – struck down and dumbfounded by the balmy bliss of springtime at early evening.

But I have somewhere I need to walk to – a place not too far out of town, perhaps half an hour's walk on my long legs; a place where something stirs in the warm twilight, emerges silently into the sun's last golden beams. I close the large, heavy doors of the bakery, and walk out into the world like a mole, eyes asquint, nose a-sneeze in the exotic air.

The sun on my face this evening is like the warm duvet I awoke in this morning – both are painful to leave. A wood pigeon coos away on some distant ledge – its timeless rep-etition comforting and sounding bizarrely – as someone once wrote – like "take two cows, Susan; take twooo cows, Susan". This, I think, is a potent sound; the auditory equivalent, perhaps, of smelling woodsmoke. Both mean "all is well in this old world".

Before long I've left the town and am wandering along a private trail; a snaking, winding path that leads to a secret corner of the marsh. Soon it will be overgrown with bramble and nettle, but for now the way ahead is clear. The air here, in this no-man's-land of slate heaps re-wilded by shrub, is thick with the incense of blossom: the coconut of gorse, the sweet milk of blackthorn. Somewhere in this small riparian jungle a cuckoo is singing his vernal love song.

I reach the river and enter the quiet gorge. Along the dead-leaf deer track that twists through a green sea of ransoms and spears of stitchwort leaves; over and under logs, past a grey-white bed of freshly plucked down. Across the river, atop the steep slope, a row of oaks is glowing gold in the dying light. I stop suddenly and hold my breath: there by the bank, a dark thing silking through the water and climbing out on to a small mud beach to rootle about, before slipping back into its element. An otter. Spirit of the river. A liquid vector moving out into deeper water; a glossy back arching up and diving down in a movement as fluid as the slow-breaking of a wave. Then it rises up, much closer now – munching its mustelid molars on a mussel or minnow. I go to step closer, to get a better view, but somehow stop myself, remembering all those times I said I'd learnt my lesson: never lose sight of it, never second guess it, never be greedy; just stay dead-still, and pray for it to move, by chance, towards you.

And it does. Closer and closer, stepping out on the muddy bank in front of me, obscured by shadow and gnarled roots of willow. Its small badger-like face still for a second, then glancing left and right; its nose twitching – something isn't right. Is it the absence of birdsong here? A strange smell? Or simply an uneasy feeling deep in its oily gut? It stares straight at me, or through me, its wild face alert, on guard. But I too am deep in shadow and shrub and nearly invisible. Then it's gone, vanished into the dusk, dissolved like a silent ghost into the inky water, and I am alone in the quiet gorge once more.

Otters, by river island, 16/04/16

Such a tiny thing,
Taming the water,
Daughter in the wake of mother.

Two slender shadows,
Rootling the shore,
In the clear moon air of April.

I was an otter,
In another age.

Now I spy on my family
From the banks of these quiet fields,
Until they vanish again into the night.

MAY IN THE MWLDAN GORGE

All is in leaf now. The stitchwort is out, the ferns are unfurling and standing erect, cleavers and nettles and brambles carpet the banks, and will soon give way to clogging walls of hemlock, cow parsley and meadowsweet. Three Welsh poppies appear anomalously in a glade, their crinkled yellow paper petals nodding in the breeze. A blade of grass holds droplets of water like peas in a pod. Cascades of honeysuckle leaves overhang the stream, sending out thirsty tendrils to sip and suck on the Mwldan. And round the bend, bluebells, dense and different amid the gorge's soft riot of green.

I set my camera trap up in the gorge, and capture the comings and goings of otters, squirrels, mice and blackbirds – the light of secret moments, sometimes blurred, snatched and set in binary code, ready to be re-glimpsed a day later by vernal voyeurs.

The chlorophyll canopy grows denser. After five weeks without rain, the heavens open briefly, and on Sunday the

14th of May – Dylan Thomas Day – the "green fuse" is fully charged, spring reaches its apex, and rumours of exhaustion and decay are already being whispered in the woods. Now is the time of new nettles. Where two weeks ago thoroughfare was granted, the way ahead is now hampered by waist-high stingers. In their shadows stitchwort, so perfectly white last week, is withering, and so too are the bluebells – already the dye has faded from their blouses; their leaves have flopped and are starting to yellow in the shade of the woodland giants which drown out the light: sycamore, ash and oak.

The pennywort leaves in the old quarry look dusty and limp. A month ago these succulent satellite dishes were turgid and glossy as they consumed the sun's rays. Now they've served their purpose, and asparagus-like spears have been spurred forth, and will soon flower a new generation. Already the hart's-tongue is fraying red at its edges; already the wren's nest is empty. The early-purple orchids on the ash log have seen better days. When the rain comes again, it patters on the woodland roof, and drips from sodden leaves. The Mwldan rises, licks loose mud from the banks, and clouds itself with pale pigments.

In the meadow above the gorge, almighty green swords guard yellow iris flowers, unfurling their first fresh petals which cloak dark stamens from the rain. Soft rush, castles of bramble, and by the water, wild mint. To be out in the rain, toward dusk, in this field burdened by green.

Returning home, after weeks of acquainting ourselves, I finally manage to feed a carrot to the skittish horse that guards the gorge. Vetch and speedwell are out now beside the stile. Wet lanes, littered with hawthorn blossom, decorated by stoic campion, lined with plantain probing upwards like outstretched boom microphones awaiting comment from the silent sky.

On the southern slope, wet with springs, cotton-grass trembles in the breeze like tufts of white wool snagged on wire. Other water-loving flowers abound here: Ragged-Robin, bogbean, purple loosestrife, marsh-marigold; horsetails form forests of miniature primeval conifers. At the field's edge, under the cover of blossoming hawthorn and bare sloe, where the horses sleep, the first of the foxgloves have let down their drawbridges and await the bees. The flowers of the ground ivy are gone. Here the elder trees, tufted with moss, have sent out green umbels, which any day will open up to reveal their gift of creamy petals and waft their savoury odour out over the paddock ("...the elder scent that is like food", as Edward Thomas put it). The air is close and thick today, filled too with the squawking of rooks.

I make convincing lists until the orchids, sedges and forget-me-nots, with their subtle variations and sub-species, remind me that classification isn't so simple: things cross-breed, hybrids occur, boundaries between species blur. I realise that this nonconformity is allowed – is inevitable and essential. This is life. Some things are hard to name; some things are nameless.

In the lonely Mwldan Meadow, a tribe of young bullocks have done a methodical job on the vegetation about the stream. Some clumps do remain though – of rush, nettle, hemlock. They avoid the woody nightshade, too, which in ancient times was hung around their necks as a charm to protect them from the evil eye.

One day a mist comes down and, ascending through the horse field, I see a police van pass a gate and then reverse. They wait for me. I stop to feed the horse a carrot and then approach. They ask where I've come from and whether I've seen anyone else whilst I've been out. I tell them I've been setting camera traps in the gorge and that I've seen no one, although I say that I thought I might have heard voices in the wood. I think about saying that it might just have been the stream – a thought which did indeed occur to me, but, realising that this sounds a little mad coming from a bearded, bog-trotting man, I think better of it. They drive on into the mist. I feed my friend another carrot and a pear, and lean on the gate, watching the valley fill with vapour. A man jogs past with his dog. And then an old banger of a car passes. A soft rain falls. It's all quite bizarre and beautiful, like a dream.

I spend days trying to identify the tiniest flowers I have ever seen and do not succeed. I'm not the only one who is ignorant of its name – the plant itself is not privy to its own human label. Perhaps it's *myotosis stricta*, a forget-me-not with a lavender-like appearance.

The day following the sea mist, a heatwave arrives. My camera trap records twenty-seven degrees in the shaded gorge. A certain magic evaporates in the perpendicular glaring of the sun. All becomes dry and bright and too real. The sideways, crepuscular light of cooler days is best. The Mwldan is sluggish in the meadow, appearing to remain motionless, utterly clear. Farm machines make the most of the weather in neighbouring fields, disturbing the usual tranquillity. All the plants seem tired and flaccid, and gnats buzz busily above the faster riffles.

On the lane a boy comes round the corner pulled by a horse – it's not a cart he's on, but a broken quad bike, roped to a scruffy nag. 'Looks like fun,' I say. 'I haven't taken him out since Barley Saturday,' he says. 'I'm giving him some training.' The lad, who looks to be about twelve with a cow-lick fringe, proceeds to tell me about all manner of things, while at the same time seeming only partially conscious that I'm there at all.

'I've been on holiday to Bala. It's not my favourite place. It's Gog Land up there. Well I don't exactly like Gog Land. I can't quite cooperate with it if I tell the truth.'

It turns out the horse I've been feeding is his. 'Tex, he's called. And the other is Taffy.' I tell him I've seen otters in the gorge. He tells me there aren't any. I show him a photo. He feigns interest and educates me about the bit of bog he owns, where he grows nettles to make tea: 'They're full of iron,' he says. He turns his horse into a meadow and gets it to pull him uphill and back to his farm.

At the end of May, yellow things emerge: in the paddock, bird's-foot trefoil and suckling clover; climbing in the hedges, meadow vetchling. Under a bright, waxing crescent moon, I pick elderflower in the dusk to make champagne. May is past – spring is gone; but I'll bottle a little of them up for future months, when magic is thinner on the ground.

MUSHROOMS & MYSTICS
IN THE BREFI VALLEY

Two weeks before my eighteenth birthday, I picked a hundred magic mushrooms from a glistening sheep field high in the Brefi valley and tried to dry them out on newspaper before a roaring log fire. I ate them on Halloween – still sticky with Welsh water and speckled with Cambrian grass – at a Zombie Ball, and came close, I think, to losing my mind. I was seeking rapid escape from mental health problems – namely paranoia and OCD – and in the process inevitably stoked the fire of illness further. Don't blow on flames you wish to extinguish. If you open the mind up wide, both the light and the dark will enter.

Two or three years before, I had found Osho in the very same valley, in the form of books lent by friends who lived in a stone cottage on a steep hillside at the end of a bumpy track. I loved that home, and its inhabitants, and the warm apple juice with cinnamon they made for me; the magical Jacob's Ladder, with its ribbons of silk, which went on folding over itself again and again; the wood-burner, and the vast view of the Brefi valley with its giant landslips of scree, and the jets that boomed by far below us.

The Brefi, then, a decade and more ago, somehow bestowed upon me the makings of a riddle and the makings of an answer: the riddle of madness and sadness and darkness; the answer of sanity and joy and light. But before I could make sense of my multi-coloured mind, which went spinning round in cycles of illusion, I would have to learn a bit about its form and function – much like the Jacob's Ladder I had played with as a child in that house.

During this whole project which has currently lasted six years, I have not visited the Brefi, nor paid much attention to the fact that both the mushrooms and the guru, in a deep way, are responsible for my love of rivers; are responsible for who I am today. Now, as I near the end of the book, I see how an exploration of these ideas and happenings is integral, essential – constitutes, even, the elusive thread that adds context to these disparate wonderings and wanderings.

Seeking guidance and solace in the dark, wintry months following my trip in October 2007, I began to reread Osho, and came across various sections detailing his own love affairs with rivers:

"The first thing my own father taught me – and the only thing that he ever taught me – was a love for the small river that flows by the side of my town. He taught me just this – swimming in the river. That's all that he ever taught me, but I am tremendously grateful to him because that brought so many changes in my life. Exactly like Siddhartha, I fell in love with the river."[16]

From my new home in Buckfastleigh, I began to explore the valleys and hills and forests of the surrounding moors. Inevitably the River Dart became for me a gateway into Dartmoor's heart. It skirted my small town, and travelled through my home town of Totnes (indeed, it was here, on an island near the centre of Totnes, that I came face to face with madness, as I teetered above the Dart's swollen, midnight waters) – and yet I did not know its source, nor its moorland course. So I began to trace its journey, to learn its secret meanderings, and in doing so, I began to ask why I myself was not skinny-dipping in its secret pools and meditating on its green banks, just as Osho had done in his youth.

I realised that, although my mind was out of balance – unwell – my body was in its prime. I couldn't take this for granted, and needed to cherish it and utilise it to release myself from the mind games I had become stuck in. Osho's message made me remember to take responsibility for who I was, to strive for greater self-understanding, to make the most of having a healthy body, to remember the "watcher on the hill".

....

[16] Osho, *Autobiography of a Spiritually Incorrect Mystic* (New York: St. Martin's Griffin, 2000), p.38.

For me that meant experiencing nature and learning about myself through solitude and silence. One day I walked high into the moors, took off all my clothes, and waded out into a wide green pool. My first wild skinny-dip. It was just a swim in a river, but that occasion marked something important for me: I was able to help myself – I had found something of real value; I could be self-sufficient and independent; in the river I had found a new world, in which I could possibly find myself.

Ten years ago today I ate mushrooms from this valley and in doing so began a journey – a journey which in a sense has led me to rivers, to the Teifi, to my life as it is now. I came up here today to Cwm Brefi hoping to see my old friends in their house high on the wild hillside, hoping to reminisce about the old days, about mushrooms and mystics, but they are not at home. Everything changes, nothing stands still. I traipse back to my car through the very fields from which I harvested my hallucinogenic hoard, and consider picking a single homeopathic 'shroom to mark the occasion, but decide against it. The land itself is my medicine now; the slow passing of time, forever opening onto the present, is my cure. Today is Halloween – the veils between worlds are thin enough, no need to tempt fate. All around me, these vast, undulating hills are alive with galaxies of tiny psilocybin-bearing fruits which could send one tripping to the outer reaches of the cosmos.

I've already had my share. I sit on a bridge over the Brefi and listen to its cold gurgling, and give thanks for the world I live in now.

it all began here,
and here it all ends.
the way the mind
bends the river;
the way the river
mends the mind.

In 2001 **Ian Phillips** moved away from a career as an illustrator in London to mid-Wales, to study the landscape and improve his printmaking. Since then he has been creating sequential series of large-scale landscape and seascape linocuts, utilising all the inspiring mark-making, pattern and techniques he has absorbed over the years from a wide variety of sources. He has attended a residency with artists from the Torres Strait Islands at Djumbunji Print workshop in Cairns, studied with Professor Wang Chou in Hangzhou, China, and worked with the Pine Feroda print collaboration. Phillips now specialises in prints based on drawing long distance walks and exploring areas of iconic interest and lonely beauty.

ACKNOWLEDGEMENTS

All reasonable efforts have been made to trace the authors of the quotes used within *Riverwise*.

Thanks are given to the following:

Copyright © 2013 by Wendell Berry from *This Day*. Reprinted by kind permission of Counterpoint Press.

Copyright © 2010 by Seamus Heaney from *Human Chain*. Reprinted by kind permission of Faber & Faber.

Copyright © 1976 by N Scott Momaday from *The Way to Rainy Mountain*. Reprinted by kind permission of University of New Mexico Press.

Copyright © 2011 by Nan Shepherd from *The Living Mountain*. Reprinted by kind permission of Canongate Books.

Copyright © A Geological background for planning and development in the Afon Teifi catchment, by R A Waters, J R Davies, D Wilson and J K Prigmore. Reprinted by kind permission of the British Geological Survey.

Copyright © 1974 by J Geraint Jenkins from *Nets and Coracles,* (David & Charles). Reprinted by kind permission of the author and publisher.

Copyright © *OSHO: Autobiography of a Spiritually Incorrect Mystic*. Reprinted by kind permission of the Osho International Foundation.

Thank you Carly for your tireless support and expertise in bringing *Riverwise* to fruition, and also for so clearly understanding, and sharing, my vision for the book. It has been a delight to have you as my editor.

Thank you Rich and Gill for saying yes, and taking a punt on the Teifi.

Thank you Seren for putting up with this ongoing extramarital affair – more than that: for encouraging my river-love and my small pilgrimages.

Thank you Ian for gracing these pages with your stunning, animistic prints.

Thank you Lisa Hellier for the gorgeous map.

Thank you Alex for once asking me if I was happy with this book. You prompted three more years of wanderings and writings.

Thank you Rachel Burdett (previously Sherratt) for publishing a short story of mine in the school magazine when I was fourteen. This small act made me want to be a writer.

Thank you to each and every one of you who features in this book: you are part and parcel of the Teifi and her land.